Michelangelo

D1576801

Michelangelo

ELENA CAPRETTI

D&C

David and Charles

Graphic design: Franco Bulletti; *Editorial Manager:* Claudio Pescio
Editors: Dario Dondi, Ilaria Ferraris and Laura Lari
English Translation: Julia Hanna Weis; *Layout:* Elisabet Ribera
Picture research: Cristina Reggioli and Valentina Gailli

The entries in the chapters on *Architecture*, pages 386-387 and from page 408 to page 425, on the Drawings, from page 596 to page 623 and Poems from page 626 to page 635, are by Elisabetta Morici. The chapter on the artist's Life is a revision of Enrica Crispino's text published in Michelangelo in the Vita d'Artista series published by Giunti in 2001. Some of the entries on the works of art are based on essays that appeared in the Dossiers: Michelangelo. The Early Years by C. Acidini Luchinat, E. Capretti, K. Weil-Garris Brandt; Michelangelo. The David, by A. Paolucci, G. M. Radke, F. Falletti; Michelangelo. The Last Judgment, by F. Mancinelli, G. Colalucci, N. Gabrielli; Michelangelo. Sculpture, by G. Cosmo, all published by Giunti.

www. giunti.it

A DAVID & CHARLES BOOK

David & Charles is an F+W
Publications Inc. company
4700 East Galbraith Road
Cincinnati, OH 45236

First published in the UK in 2006
© 2006 Ministero per i Beni e le Attività
Culturali – Soprintendenza Speciale per il
Polo Museale Fiorentino

© 2006 Giunti Editore S.p.A.
Via Bolognese 165 - 50139 Florence
Via Dante 4 - 20121 Milan

"FIRENZE MVSEI" is a registered
trademark created by Sergio Bianco

A catalogue record for this book
is available from the British Library.

ISBN-13: 978-0-7153-2675-6 hardback
ISBN-10: 0-7153-2675-9 hardback

Printed in Great Britain by Butler & Tanner
for David & Charles
Brunel House   Newton Abbot
Devon

Visit our website at
www.davidandcharles.co.uk

David & Charles books are
available from all good bookshops;
alternatively you can contact our
Orderline on 0870 9908222
or write to us at FREEPOST
EX2 110, D&C Direct, Newton
Abbot, TQ12 4ZZ (no stamp
required UK only); US customers
call 800-289-0963 and Canadian
customers call 800-840-5220.

Contents

MICHELAGNOLO BVONAR. PIT.
SCVLTORE ET ARCHITET.

Life

Caprese, Settignano and Florence. Most of what we know about Michelangelo's life comes from the two biographies written during his lifetime: one by Giorgio Vasari, from 1550 and updated in the second edition of 1568, and another by Ascanio Condivi (1553). The latter, who was one of Michelangelo's pupils claimed that his text was completely truthful and reliable even though it was written under the master's close supervision and most probably wanted to highlight some episodes, gloss over others and even conceal information about certain works, especially those from his early years that did not reflect his mature style. Other information about the artist's life comes from his letters to family members with whom he always maintained close ties.

Michelangelo was born on 6 March 1475 at Caprese (today the town is known as Caprese Michelangelo), not far from Arezzo. Son of Ludovico di Leonardo Buonarroti Simoni and Francesca di Neri di ser Miniato del Sera, he was the second of four children. According to Condivi the child was born under a lucky star, with "Mercury and Venus in the second house of Jupiter." The planet Jupiter is the protector of creativity and would help him succeed in "any undertaking, but mainly the arts which delight the senses, such as painting, sculpture and architecture." His father, Ludovico, was the podesta, that is the chief

magistrate, of Caprese and nearby Chiusi for the Florentine Republic. Michelangelo would always be proud of belonging to the lesser nobility which, though not wealthy, boasted of descending from Matilde di Canossa. Ludovico's mandate expired and shortly after the child's birth the family moved back to their native city, Florence. Little Michelangelo was given to a wet-nurse at Settignano, a nearby village where the Buonarroti family had an estate with a villa. The woman who nursed him was both the daughter and wife of stone cutters, the craft that brought the village its fame. According to Condivi, Michelangelo said that "he suckled hammers and chisels with his nurse's milk". In 1481, the six-year old lost his mother, it was a loss that would mark him for the rest of his life.

On page 8,
Portrait of Michelangelo,
woodcut from
Vasari's *Lives*
1568 edition.
This page,
the house where
Michelangelo was
born at Caprese
(Arezzo).

Opposite page,
the church
at Caprese.

Against his father's wishes he embarked on a career in art. Sometime around 1485 Ludovico sent his ten year-old son to Francesco da Urbino's grammar school to begin his studies of letters and the law. Michelangelo did learn to write, but could care less about Greek and Latin and took time from his studies to practice drawing and mingle with painters; in the end he finally obtained his father's permission to devote himself to art.

The workshop of Domenico Ghirlandaio. Michelangelo began his artistic training with painting. He became very close friends with Francesco Granacci who was six years his senior and recognized the young boy's special talents. He encouraged him to follow his instincts and helped him practice and acquire experience. Indeed, Granacci introduced him to his own former teacher, the painter Domenico Ghirlandaio who shared a prestigious atelier with his brother. Twelve-year old Michelangelo began his apprenticeship with the Ghirlandaio brothers, Domenico and David, in June 1487. His contract was for three years, but – and it seems due to conflicts with the master – he left the atelier at the end of the first year. It was probably thanks to the Ghirlandaio brothers who were then decorating the choir in Santa Maria Novella that Michelangelo had his first contact with the fresco technique. During that period Michelangelo practiced drawing, and "for many months" (Vasari) copied the works of past Florentine masters such as Giotto and Masaccio, and artists from northern Europe as borne out by informa-

Copy (c. 1490)
of a figure from
the *Ascension of Saint John
the Evangelist* by Giotto,
in Santa Croce; Paris,
Louvre, Département
des Arts Graphiques.

Copy (1488-1495)
of a figure from
the *Tribute Money*
by Masaccio; Munich,
Kupferstichkabinett.

tion concerning a lost painting done after an engraving by Martin Schongauer. Michelangelo continued to draw over the following years. Once, when he was in the Brancacci Chapel in Santa Maria del Carmine, intent on copying Masaccio's frescoes along with other young apprentices, his drawings aroused the uncontrollable envy of Pietro Torrigiano who punched him soundly in the nose. Torrigiano paid for his angry gesture by being banished from Florence.

The San Marco Garden. Between 1489 and 1490 Michelangelo met the man who would definitely influence his life; the man was Lorenzo the Magnificent and the meeting occurred in his "sculpture garden" at San Marco. It is uncertain as to whether it was Granacci who took his friend to the garden as Condivi maintains, or whether the Ghirlandaio brothers pointed out their promising pupil to Lorenzo, which is Vasari's version. The fact is that this was Michelangelo's first opportunity to try his hand at what would be his preferred art, sculpture. Lorenzo de' Medici, the lord of Florence from 1469, was known as The Magnificent for his diplomatic and political skills and for the role he played not only as patron, but also arbiter of the arts and culture. During his lifetime he was already the symbol of XV century Florence and of the Italian Renaissance in general. The Tuscan capital reached its maximum splendor under Lorenzo, dominating not only Italy, but most of Europe, on the economic and cultural horizons. A man of letters and a

Giorgio Vasari and helpers,
*Lorenzo the Magnificent
with the Philosophers and Scholars
of His Day*, 1555-1562;
Florence, Palazzo Vecchio.

Ottavio Vannini,
*Lorenzo de' Medici
and the Artists
in the Sculpture
Garden,*
1638-1642;
Florence, Palazzo
Pitti, Museo
degli Argenti,
Salone di Giovanni
da San Giovanni.

poet himself, he collected valuable objects and ancient statues, in brief, the Magnificent sponsored the arts and letters to a high degree. Illustrious men such as Luigi Pulci, Agnolo Poliziano, Marsilio Ficino, Cristoforo Landino and Pico della Mirandola lived and worked with him; the greatest artists of the era were in his service. Some of them also worked at other Italian courts and were practically Lorenzo's cultural ambassadors: Botticelli – leading representative of the period's figurative style, Antonio Pollaiolo, Andrea Verrocchio, Domenico Ghirlandaio and the young Leonardo.

The garden of San Marco was located near the Dominican monastery of the same name, built by Cosimo the Elder, Lorenzo's grandfather, about forty years earlier. The garden was in the heart of the Medici district on Via Larga (today's Via Cavour) where the Medici palace also stood. Lorenzo had brought a collection of valuable ancient statues and inscriptions, perhaps in need of restoration, along with some XV century works (especially drawings) to this place. The Medici property comprised two buildings and two outdoor areas. One of the buildings was the headquarters of the Confraternity of the Magi. Sources also tell of buildings with "loggia," "bed-

Detail
of the *Map of Florence*
by Stefano Buonsignori, 1584:
1. Palazzo Medici
2. San Marco
3. Medici Garden

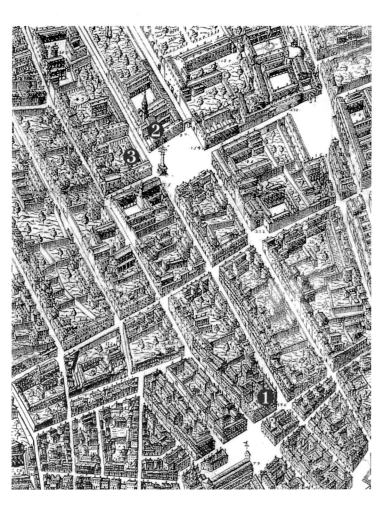

rooms" and "kitchen" inside the complex which is also mentioned as a restoration workshop, the venue for banquets and performances as well as the yard where the decorations for the spectacular processions and pageants held in the city were built. It was also where the stone cutters worked on roughing the stones to be used in the construction of a library that Lorenzo wanted to build in the San Lorenzo complex (a project that had been shelved for many years and then, as we shall see, was completed by Michelangelo himself).

The "garden" was open to artists and visitors from at least 1475 on, that is when Leonardo joined the group. The young men's teacher, and conservator of the collection, was Bertoldo, a former assistant to Donatello and friend of the Magnificent whom he accompanied during his stays at spas. Vasari wrote: "At that time the Magnificent Lorenzo de' Medici kept the sculptor Bertoldo in his garden on the Piazza di S. Marco, not so much as custodian or guardian of the many beautiful antiques that he had collected and gathered together at great expense in that place, as because, desiring very earnestly to create a school of excellent painters and sculptors, he wished that these should have as their chief and guide the above-named Bertoldo, who was a disciple of Donato." The garden of San Marco was neither a school in the academic sense nor an artisan workshop. Rather, it was a gymnasium of the mind in the generic sense of a stimulating place where talented young men could meet artists and literati, but above all could talk and work in front of ancient statuary – drawing, copying or repairing under the outstanding guidance of Bertoldo, the last heir of the great Donatello's teachings. The garden was also an important focus for the dissemination and promotion of Laurentian cultural policy. Lorenzo certainly must have counted considerably on the "nursery of talents." Indeed, it seems that he supported those who frequented the garden by paying them salaries and bonuses.

When Michelangelo was taken to the garden of San Marco around 1489 he found other boys who, like himself, had been admitted to study the prestigious Medici collection. Among these were the sculptors Pietro Torrigiano, Giovanfrancesco Rustici, Baccio da Montelupo, Andrea Sansovino and the painters Niccolò Soggi, Lorenzo di Credi and Giuliano Bugiardini. There, at San Marco Michelangelo discovered his true calling, sculpture. While he practiced on sculptures in the garden and began learning the stone carvers' craft, Bertoldo introduced Michelangelo to the study of ancient models and probably to terracotta, plaster and bronze, the technique in which Bertoldo excelled. Thus we can suppose that during those years Michelangelo experimented carving wood and marble elsewhere. His earliest experience with marble may have been under the guidance of Benedetto da Maiano who had been working on the marble altarpiece of the Annunciation for the church of Sant'Anna dei Lombardi in Naples since 1489. In fact, the *putto* holding the garland on the right of the altar frontal has been attributed to Michelangelo.

Piazza San Marco today:
the cypress trees on the right
are where the Medici
sculpture garden once was.

Opposite page,
Palazzo Medici Riccardi
in Florence.

Michelangelo's rendezvous with destiny occurred there, in the San Marco garden. A stroke of luck brought the young artist under the personal protection of Lorenzo. The story of how the two met is one of the most famous anecdotes reported by sources on the sculptor's youth. Walking through the garden, Lorenzo de' Medici saw a marble "head of a faun". It was the young Michelangelo who had carved it, copying an ancient, timeworn sculpture of an old, leering faun. Most impressed, the Magnificent good-naturedly teased the aspiring artist because of the too perfect teeth he had made for the old mouth. Left alone, Michelangelo hastily and boldly modified his statue, removing one of the teeth and drilling into the gums to make it look "as if it had come out by the root," as Condivi put it. When Lorenzo returned, he congratulated the boy. He then spoke to Michelangelo's father and convinced him to allow him to host the boy in his palace in Via Larga where he would raise and educate him with his own children. It was one of those opportunities that only comes once in a lifetime, and Michelangelo did not let it get away. Even his father Ludovico, who at first was against the idea, could benefit from the situation by getting some support from the Medici for his own business.

There is no trace of that *Faun*. However, some believed that there was a copy of it in a mask, (now lost) that had been conserved in the Museo Nazionale del Bargello in Florence. The piece may have inspired Ottavio Vannini when he painted the scene of Lorenzo the Magnificent and the Young Michelangelo in the Pitti Palace (1638-1642).

Copy (Florence, Casa Buonarroti) of the head of a *Faun* formerly in the Museo Nazionale del Bargello and attributed to Michelangelo, since lost.

Master close to Bertoldo and Michelangelo, *Bust of a Satyr*, late XV century; Florence, Museo Nazionale del Bargello.

At the Medici's. The young Michelangelo's talent matured quickly in Lorenzo's milieu. For Buonarroti entrance to the Medici palace meant continuous contact with the most cultured men of the times: with Poliziano who was tutor to Lorenzo's sons, with Marsilio Ficino and Girolamo Benivieni and with Pico della Mirandola. It also meant having access to the priceless pieces in the palace, the gems, medals, jewels and other rare, valuable items that the Magnificent collected and which had a decisive influence on the artist's development.

Thanks to Lorenzo and his refined entourage, Michelangelo was able to experience the impact that classical antiquity exerted on art and culture in Florence from the earliest decades of the century. Tangible proof of this was the practice of collecting curiosities, manuscripts, sculptures, semiprecious stone vases, gems and cameos of which Lorenzo was the unsurpassed master, proving his tenacity, open-mindedness and intellectual clarity.

Michelangelo had the opportunity to see the architectural achievements of Alberti and Brunelleschi, sculptures by Donatello and his pupils (such as Bertoldo) the mythological paintings by Piero di Cosimo, Pollaiolo and Botticelli, to hear and read the literary compositions by Poliziano "[...] as everyone knows, a man whose man learning and brilliance is fully revealed in his writings..." (Condivi). At the Medici court the classics took on new nuances thanks to the influence of the philosophical theories of Marsilio Ficino, a scholar and divulgator of Plato's works. At the base of this thought was the aim of recon-

Carnelian, from the Laurentian
collection, known as the
Seal of Nero by Dioscurides,
I century B.C.; Naples,
Museo Archeologico Nazionale.

ciling Christianity and Platonism. Hence the massive influx of Neoplatonic motifs in the artistic production of the Laurentian circle and the birth of particular hybrids: works in which complex Neoplatonic meanings overlapped themes and subjects drawn from the classical repertory such as the pagan allegories depicted by Sandro Botticelli, in the *Allegory of Spring* and the *Birth of Venus*. The experiences gained in the garden of San Marco, life in the Magnificent's palace on Via Larga, the meetings and erudite discussions with the artists and literati of the Medici entourage, yielded their first original results between 1490 and 1492 when Michelangelo carved two marble relief sculptures, the *Madonna of the Stairs* and the *Battle of the Centaurs*. If in the first the young artist revealed his debt to Donatello, in the second he put his personal imprint on a reinterpretation of ancient and modern works dealing with the same subject – from Ro-

Kneeling Female Nude
(study for the *Entombment*),
c. 1500-1501; Paris, Louvre,
Département des Arts Graphiques.

man sarcophagi at the Camposanto (cemetery) in Pisa, to Giovanni Pisano's marble pulpits, some of Antonio del Pollaiolo's creations (such as the engraving with the *Battle of the Nudes*) and the bronze relief of the *Battle of the Romans and Barbarians* by Bertoldo, now in the Bargello. In these two "early works" Buonarroti's style was already very personal and profoundly different from that of the other sculptors on the Florentine artistic scene such as Verrocchio, Andrea del Pollaiolo or Andrea Sansovino, and he also started to distance himself from the language of his two presumed teachers, Bertoldo di Giovanni and Benedetto da Maiano.

The Death of Lorenzo the Magnificent; Piero the Unfortunate, Savonarola. Lorenzo de' Medici died in 1492 at the age of forty-two. America was discovered that same year and the two concomitant events seemed to symbolically mark the end of one era and the beginning of another. Michelangelo lost his first great protector and patron. Desolate, the young artist went back to live with his father for a time, but was soon summoned back to the Palazzo Medici by Lorenzo's eldest son, Piero, known as

Opposite page, above:
Antonio Pollaiolo,
Battle of the Nudes,
c. 1460; Chiari (Brescia),
Fondazione Morcelli-Repossi.

Bertoldo di Giovanni,
Battle Scene, c. 1479,
detail; Florence, Museo
Nazionale del Bargello.

"the unfortunate." It happened on the occasion of the great snowstorm on 20 January 1494. Surprised by the unusual white blanket covering the city, and to satisfy a childish whim – he wanted a snowman in his palace courtyard – Piero summoned Michelangelo to build it, and then invited to stay at the palace as he had in the past. The relationship between Buonarroti and the Medici was difficult and filled with misunderstandings, at least according to the biographers, especially Condivi who defined the Magnificent's first son as "insolent and supercilious," and so inept as to consider Michelangelo the equal of his handsome Spanish footman.

Circle of Andrea
Verrocchio,
*Bust of Lorenzo
the Magnificent*,
c. 1492;
Washington,
National Gallery.

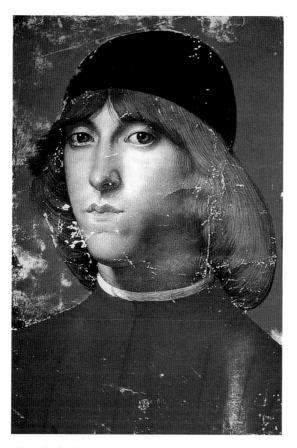

Gherardo di Giovanni,
Piero di Lorenzo de' Medici,
1489; Naples,
Biblioteca Nazionale.

Michelangelo continued working in the garden of San Marco. There, between 1492 and 1494, perhaps on the request of Piero himself, he carved a *Hercules* from a block of marble over 2 meters high. This, the first of Michelangelo's monumental sculptures, became the property of the Strozzi family and then, after several vicissitudes, ended up in France in the gardens of the Fontainebleau palace from where it disappeared some time after 1725.

In the meantime Michelangelo also began frequenting the monastery of Santo Spirito, where the cultural interests of the avant-garde groups capable of anticipating the times had long been fueled. There, Francesco Petrarch and Giovanni Boccaccio had both found comfort in the cells of the Augustinian monks, while at the end of the XIV century Fra' Luigi Marsili had gathered around him the first humanistic circles. Michelangelo was welcomed there by the prior, Niccolò Bicchielli who allowed him to study anatomy by dissecting the corpses buried in the complex. Out of gratitude Michelangelo carved a wooden *Crucifix* that the prior placed over the altar in the magnificent church Brunelleschi had designed fifty years earlier. Believed lost for a long time, today the majority of scholars believes that it is the *Crucifix* that was found in the monastery in 1962 and today, after careful restorations and studies, it is displayed in the sacristy. The intense spirituality of that thin, fragile body reflects the teachings of Fra' Girolamo Savonarola, prior of the Dominican monastery of San Marco who, for some time had been preaching a return to a rigorous and austere religious art

Fra' Bartolomeo,
Portrait of Girolamo Savonarola,
c. 1499-1500;
Florence, Museo di San Marco.

that would arouse sincere sense of mercy in the faithful. For Savonarola the crucifix was a privileged theme of devotion as were its artistic portrayals, and so he favored production of such pieces for private use and worship. In this climate and under such influence Michelangelo may have carved other crucifixes, including one of linden wood, datable around 1495, that is in a private collection, and was recently attributed to him.

In the meantime, Girolamo Savonarola's rousing, visionary sermons were becoming very popular throughout Florence, bringing the Dominican monk and his ideas for radical reform more and more approval and praise while a climate of great political tension was developing. In the midst of the economic crisis, there was an increasing desire for a political, social, cultural and spiritual renewal with the aim of recovering old ethical and religious values that seemed to have been suffocated in and by Lorenzo's sophisticated and opulent society. After the Magnificent's death, the political situation throughout Italy was once again unstable. The particularisim of the several Italian city-states and the shortsightedness of their rulers led to the invasion by Charles VIII, King of France in 1494, that marked the beginning of foreign expansion in Italy. The descent of the French king had very important consequences for Florence as it led to the downfall of the Medici regime. Piero de' Medici had decided to maintain the traditional alliance with the King of Naples, Ferdinando II, against whom Charles VIII was moving and claiming his dynastic rights to the throne occupied

Crucifix,
c. 1495;
private collection.

by the House of Aragon; so the Florentines were filled with apprehension as Charles' troops advanced. When Charles VIII reached the outskirts of Florence, Lorenzo's son ineptitude in dealing with the foreign king – accepting a humiliating surrender – led to the outbreak of an insurrection led by Savonarola who, on 9 November 1494, forced Piero to flee the city with his family, and established a republican government with widespread popular representation. The Dominican monk was the inspiring force of the new republic devoted to the Savior as the sole sovereign of the city, whose will was expressed via the Great Council, that met in Palazzo della Signoria and was established as the basis of the new order.

Between Florence and Bologna. Many of Michelangelo's teachers and protectors also died around the same time as that Lorenzo the Magnificent died. Bertoldo passed away in 1491 at the Villa of Poggio a Caiano, in 1494 it was Domenico Ghirlandaio and on 29 September 1494 Agnolo Poliziano breathed his last in his home that was just a short distance from the "sculpture" gardens. For Michelangelo it meant the loss of people who had been important references during his youth. While tension and discontent were rising, in October 1494 – about one month before the revolt led by Savonarola – Michelangelo, like several of his companions from the garden of San Marco, left Florence, incurring the wrath of Piero de' Medici. According to Condivi, the artist had been prompted to flee mainly because of a series of visions that

Donatello, *David*,
fourth decade
of the XV century;
Florence, Museo
Nazionale del Bargello.

a court musician, known as Cardiere, had had in his dreams: he said that he repeatedly saw the dead Lorenzo the Magnificent dressed in ragged black foretelling Piero about his banishment from Florence.

Michelangelo went to Venice where stayed only a few days and then returned to Bologna where he was the guest of Gianfrancesco Aldrovandi, trusted advisor to Giovanni Bentivoglio, ruler of the city and friend of the Medici. In fact, just then Piero de' Medici was asking Bentivoglio for help against the French and would soon be requesting hospitality for himself and his family en route to exile in Venice. According to Condivi, Aldrovandi helped Buonarroti who was stopped at the *Ufficio delle Bullette* because he did not have enough money to pay the fee to enter the city. As a guest of Aldrovandi Michelangelo entertained his host in the evenings by reading from Dante, Petrarch and Boccaccio. While he was taking advantage of his sojourn to study Ferrarese painting, Michelangelo was asked to participate in the competition for the marble tomb of Saint Dominic in the church dedicated to the saint that had been begun by Nicola Pisano in 1265-1267.

For the monument Michelangelo made the *Angel with a Candelabrum* as a companion to the one by Niccolò dell'Arca, the *Saint Petronius* and *San Proculus*. It is likely that while in Bologna he met with Giovanni and Giuliano de' Medici, Piero's younger brothers who arrived there on 14 November 1495 during their escape from Florence to Milan. Just a few days earlier, Giovanni Bentivoglio had

Tomb of Saint Dominic,
XIII-XVI century; Bologna,
Basilica of San Domenico.

purchased the garden of San Marco in Florence that had been confiscated by the newly founded republic.

Around Christmas of 1495 Michelangelo returned to Florence where the republican government was getting organized and Savonarola's fiery words were resounding louder than ever. They were words that inevitably touched even the sensitive and receptive artist. Back in his city, Michelangelo got in touch with Lorenzo di Pierfrancesco de' Medici, young second cousin to Lorenzo the Magnificent. Piero the Unfortunate had sent Lorenzo junior and his brother Giovanni into exile after the Magnificent's death. The young Lorenzo returned to Florence following the arrival of King Charles VIII of Anjou after Piero de' Medici and his family had been banished in November 1494. At that time both brothers had taken the appellative of *Popolano,* "of the people." For Lorenzo di Pierfrancesco, Michelangelo completed a marble statue of the *Young Saint John* that he may have started prior to his departure for Bologna. This statue – that has since been lost – originally stood in the "old" Medici residence on Via Larga close to the XV century palazzo where Lorenzo the Magnificent and Piero the Unfortunate had lived. In a room with a Medieval imprint there were exquisite furnishings and famous artworks such as a *Tondo* by Signorelli and Botticelli's *Allegory of Spring.* Lorenzo junior also owned the latter's *Birth of Venus* which he kept in the country estate at Castello. It was probably Lorenzo di Pierfrancesco who suggested the swindle of the *Sleeping Cupid:* it was a stat-

Above, Francesco Granacci,
*Entrance of Charles VIII into
Florence*, second decade of the
XVI century; Florence, Uffizi.

Below,
Sandro Botticelli,
Allegory of Spring,
c. 1482; Florence, Uffizi.

Andrea Verrocchio,
David, c. 1465;
Florence, Museo
Nazionale del Bargello.

Opposite page,
sketch for the bronze
David, 1501-1502;
Paris, Louvre,
Département
des Arts Graphiques.

45

ue by Michelangelo that so closely resembled an ancient sculpture that it could be passed for an archeological find after having been "aged" and dirtied. In concert with Lorenzo and Michelangelo, the merchant Baldassare del Milanese who lived across from the Medici palace, sold the piece to Cardinal Raffaele Riario in Rome, saying that it had been found in an excavation, and obtained a very high price. Later, when the fraud was discovered, the cardinal sent the banker Jacopo Galli to Florence as his emissary to demand a refund and to meet the author of the piece which was of undoubted quality. All traces of Michelangelo's sculpture were lost after it entered the collection of Isabella d'Este in Mantua. Since the Gonzaga collections were sold to the English Crown in the XVII century, it is probable that Michelangelo's sculpture was destroyed along with other treasures in the Whitehall Palace fire of 1698. A *Sleeping Cupid* that is currently in the Corsham Court Collection (Wilshire) is believed to be quite similar to Michelangelo's original. And there are several other pieces inspired by Michelangelo's *Cupid,* including a painting of the *Virgin and Child*

Opposite page, above, Bartolomeo Passarotti, *Sleeping Cupid*, second half of the XVI century; Florence, Gabinetto Disegni e Stampe degli Uffizi.

Below, copies of statues of the Sleeping Cupid, from *Busts and Statues in Whitehall Garden*, XVII century; Windsor, Royal Library.

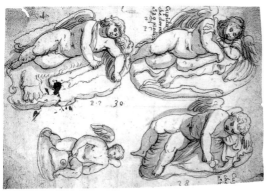

47

with Saint Ann by the artist known as Ferrando Spagnolo who had worked with Leonardo and a drawing by Bartolomeo Passarotti which is in the Uffizi.

Rome. After the invitations and urgings on the parts of Del Milanese and Cardinal Riario, Michelangelo left for Rome in June 1496, with letters of introduction signed by Lorenzo di Pierfrancesco de' Medici who was well known and respected in the pontifical city. From Republican Florence dominated by Savonarola the young sculptor – he was slightly more than twenty – reached the Rome of the popes, where the Borgia pope, Alexander VI sat on Peter's throne and was the object of the fiercest attacks by the Dominican friar.

Michelangelo had everything to gain from a sojourn in Rome. First of all, he was far from the increasingly critical climate in Florence where without a doubt – even though he admired Savonarola – the religious fanaticism made the political and social situations evermore tense and strict censorship of artistic production hindered the development of art and the flourishing of patronage. Then, being in the *Urbe* allowed him refine his technique by studying ancient sculptures first hand, thanks also to the

Sketch for a David with sling,
1501; Paris, Louvre,
Département
des Arts Graphiques.

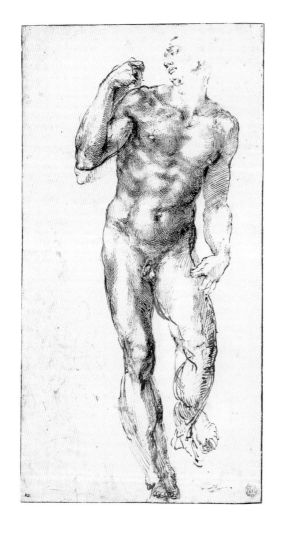

fine collections that were amassed by the rich and educated members of the Roman curia. And finally, Michelangelo could also have excellent opportunities for work and success in a city that did not yet offer him any fierce competition: the artists, such as Pinturicchio (who had frescoed the Borgia apartments in the Vatican palace) and the sculptor Andrea Bregno, were good, but certainly not outstanding. Furthermore, Michelangelo was also, doubtless, favored by the fact that he could enter the circles of Cardinal Raffaele Riario It was a milieu that included some Florentine bankers who had settled in Rome, and one of the most frequently mentioned of these was Jacopo Galli, who was very influential in Rome and offered the young Buonarroti protection and hospitality.

The banker owned a home in the city; the garden was a true outdoor "antiquarium" that housed ancient and modern artworks. Here, as we can see from a XVI century drawing by the Flemish artist Martin van Heemskerck, Galli placed Michelangelo's statue of *Bacchus*. The marble sculpture (now in the Museo del Bargello in Florence) was made for Cardinal Riario who had rejected it and left it with Galli. Here there was yet another copy by the master, known from early sources as a an *Apollo* or a *Cupid*. Recent studies tend to identify it as the *Young Archer* which is now in the French Embassy's Cooperation and Cultural Service in New York. It was again through Galli that Michelangelo obtained the commission to carve the *Pietà* for Saint Peter's Basilica for Car-

Maarten van Heemskerck,
*The Garden of the Galli
Villa in Rome*, 1532-1535;
Berlin, Kupferstichkabinett.

A helper
of Michelangelo,
Pietà, 1499(?); Rome,
Galleria Nazionale
di Arte Antica,
Palazzo Barberini.

dinal Bilhères de Lagraulas. It is the only piece he ever signed and the sculpture that established him as a great master even among his contemporaries. Jacopo Galli probably worked as an intermediary for several of Michelangelo's commissions during this first sojourn in Rome. For example he acted as guarantor for the *Vatican Pietà* and for the *Entombment of Christ,* a painting for the church of Sant'Agostino (now in the National Gallery, London). Two other paintings would date from this period: *Saint Francis receiving the Stigmata* (lost) perhaps done on the basis of the Michelangelesque cartoon by Piero Argenta of Ferrara and the *Manchester Madonna* (London, National Gallery) for which there is record of payment dated July 1497.

Siena, Florence. In March 1501 Michelangelo left Rome, probably to work on the commission for 15 statues for the *Piccolomini Altar,* a monumental marble structure by Andrea Bregno (1483-1485) in the Siena cathedral. The verbal agreements had been made in Rome, but the contract was executed on 5 June 1501 and signed by Michelangelo, the patron Cardinal Francesco Todeschini Piccolomini (who became Pope Pius III in 1503) and Jacopo Galli who, once again, was

Andrea Bregno, Piccolomini Altar,
1483-1485; Siena, Cathedral.

the guarantor. Michelangelo only made four of the fifteen statues, *Saints Peter*, *Paul*, *Pius* and *Gregory*, because more prestigious jobs kept him near Florence.

There, the situation had changed drastically. Savonarola had clashed openly with Pope Alexander VI for having repeatedly denounced the corruption of the Roman curia and was excommunicated in 1498. Abandoned by his supporters, he was hanged and then burned as a heretic in Piazza della Signoria. Florence, however, kept its republican form of government but evolved towards a more moderate version with a gonfalonier, or magistrate, who would serve for life as the representative to settle disputes within the Great Council. In 1502 Pier Soderini was elected to this office. Under his leadership artistic patronage, that had diminished during Savonarola's short tenure, was resumed with vigor in an attempt to build a new image for the Florentine Republic. In just a few years outstanding Tuscan artists, prompted by the desire to obtain important commissions poured into the city from all over Italy. Suddenly Leonardo, Michelangelo and Raphael were all there together in that enthusiastic and stimulating climate. That short, but extraordinarily cre-

Opposite page, above,
anonymous Florentine painter,
*The Execution of Savonarola
in Piazza della Signoria*, 1498,
detail; Florence,
Museo di San Marco.
We can see Donatello's *Judith*
in front of Palazzo Vecchio.

Below,
anonymous Florentine
painter, *Festa degli omaggi*,
late XVI century, detail;
Florence, Uffizi.
Here we can see the
David in its "official" place.

ative, artistic season marked the beginning of the "modern manner" as defined by Giorgio Vasari. He had acquired such fame with the *Vatican Pietà* that upon his return to Florence Michelangelo was flooded with commissions. These included the *David,* the white giant that was placed in front of the Palazzo della Signoria, the seat of the government, with great ceremony. The artist made many sculptures during that intense Florentine period: a bronze *David* (lost) for Pierre de Rohan, Marshal of France; the twelve apostles ordered by the Woolworkers' Guild for the Florence cathedral – of which he only roughed the *Saint Matthew;* the *Virgin and Child* purchased by the Mouscron family for their chapel in the church of Notre Dame in Bruges; the *Pitti* and *Taddei tondos,* named for the clients. Sometime around 1507 Michelangelo painted the famous tondo of the *Holy Family with the Young Saint John* for Agnolo and Maddalena Doni who had already had their portraits painted by Raphael.

The most important commission during this period came from Gonfalonier Pier Soderini in 1504. Michelangelo was to have frescoed the *Battle of Cascina* in the room of the Great Council – later known as the *Salone dei Cinquecento* (Hall of the Five Hundred) – in Palazzo della Signoria. A few months earlier the first government of the republic had commissioned Leonardo da Vinci to paint the *Battle of Anghiari;* the *Battle of Cascina* was to be its companion on the opposite wall. In this way Florence wanted to celebrate the past and present glory of the

On page 57,
The David Tribune
in the Galleria
dell'Accademia,
post 1903 - ante 1909.

Piazza della Signoria
and Palazzo Vecchio
with the copy of the *David*.

Above,
Study for the *Battle of Cascina*,
c. 1504-1505; Florence,
Gabinetto Disegni
e Stampe degli Uffizi.

Aristotele da Sangallo,
copy of the lost cartoon
for the *Battle of Cascina*,
c. 1504-1505; Norfolk,
Leicester Collection.

Study for the Apostles, for the *Battle of Cascina*,
and the *Bruges Madonna*, 1504-1505; Florence,
Gabinetto Disegni e Stampe degli Uffizi.

Study of Male Nude seen from the Back
for the *Battle of Cascina*, c. 1504-1505;
London, British Museum.

republic commemorating two resounding victories: against Pisa at Cascina in 1364 and against Milan at Anghiari in 1440. This challenge between the two greatest artists who were in the city at the same time was going to prove interesting, partly because there was no love lost between Michelangelo and Leonardo and they were to have worked at the same time – a duel of artists!

Their well-known rivalry is also recorded in a mid-XVI century manuscript, the *Anonimo Magliabechiano*. There we can read about the episode of a clash between the artists on a city street. The manuscript reads: "Walking along from Santa Trinita, Leonardo, together with Giovanni da Gavine [they came to…] a group of fine men who were discussing a passage from Dante, they called Leonardo and asked him to explain that passage […]. Just then Michelangelo walked by and was called by one of them. Leonardo replied: "Michelangelo will explain it to you." To Michelangelo it seemed that Leonardo was mocking him and angrily answered, "You explain it, you who made a drawing of a horse to cast in bronze [he never made equestrian statue of Francesco Sforza] that you couldn't cast and left it out of shame." Having said this he turned his back and walked on, leaving Leonardo quite red in the face."

Neither Leonardo nor Michelangelo finished their respective *Battles* for the Great Council room, they only completed studies and the cartoons. Leonardo did, however, start painting on the wall, but used an inappropriate technique that ruined it all. Michelangelo never even got to the point of taking a brush in hand. In 1506 both artists had interrupted their work: Leonardo in order to go to Milan, summoned by the French governor, Charles d'Amboise, and Michelangelo left for Rome to perform the contract he had with Pope Julius II to carve his funeral monument. They both left the life-size cartoons in Florence; the drawings were displayed and admired by all and served as study material for several generations of artists before they were lost. From the countless derivations, copies and studies of Buonarroti's cartoons we can see that the central portion of the *Battle of Cascina* was to portray the Florentine soldiers, in complex poses with sudden, leaps and bounds, rushing out of the waters of the Arno River as the enemy troops approached. The event actually lost its narrative meaning to become a pretext for a study of the individual bodies conceived in an autonomous, dynamic and sculptural manner. The cartoon for the *Battle of Cascina* was so unusual that Benvenuto Cellini defined it as the "school for the world" – however, overuse destroyed it. It was passed from hand to hand to be admired and copied, it was divided into several parts and distributed among various Italian courts to the point that it deteriorated and was finally lost.

The Rome of Julius II. Having left the work on the *Battle of Cascina* in Florence, Michelangelo went to Rome in March 1505. He had been summoned by the Della Rovere pope, Julius II, on recommendation from the Flor-

Raphael,
Portrait of Julius II,
1512; London,
National Gallery.

Laocoon,
I century A.D.,
Vatican, Musei Vaticani.

Charles de Tolnay,
Reconstructions
of Michelangelo's first
(1505) and second
(1513) plans for the
Monument to Julius II.

Charles de Tolnay,
Reconstruction
of Michelangelo's
third (1516) and fourth
(1532) plans for the
Monument to Julius II.

entine architect Giuliano da Sangallo, to build an enormous, monumental tomb. Elected to the throne of Saint Peter after the short reign of Pius III, Julius II was, *de facto* the true successor to his bitter enemy, Alexander VI of the House of Borgia.

The new pope was determined to restore hegemony to the papacy, both in the fragmented context of Italy's city states and with respect to the great European powers. In addition, he wanted to restore the city of the Vicar of Christ on Earth to its former splendor. In parallel to his military ventures with expansionistic goals, Julius II

Opposite page, Raphael, *School of Athens*, 1509-1511; Vatican, Palazzi Vaticani, Stanza della Segnatura. Left, detail of the philosopher Heraclitus a portrait of Michelangelo that Raphael added to his finished fresco after the first portion of the Sistine Chapel ceiling was unveiled (14 August 1511).

launched a far-reaching cultural policy, surrounding himself with the greatest artists of the day such as Bramante, Michelangelo and Raphael. In this case he was entirely successful and by the early years of the XVI century Rome was the cultural capital of Italy, having stripped the title from Florence that had led the Renaissance. A humanist pope, Julius cultivated his love for antiquity in harmony with the tastes of his era. His collection of classical sculptures in the Belvedere Courtyard in the Vatican was one of the most prestigious anywhere. It included famous pieces such as the *Apollo* and the *Laocoon* found

*Study for the Erythrean Sybil
on the ceiling of the Sistine
Chapel*, 1508-1512;
London, British Museum.

Opposite page,
*Study for the "Ignudo" above
the Persian Sybil on the ceiling
of the Sistine Chapel*, 1508-1512;
Haarlem, Teyler Museum.

in 1506 during an excavation of a vineyard not far from church of Santa Maria Maggiore. The discovery not only resounded through Rome's cultural milieus, but it was actually witnessed by Michelangelo who had come from Florence to see the famous group brought to light. Furthermore, in Rome – where he had already gone to see and study ancient ruins and classical monuments – during the XVI century collecting archeological finds and statues became a widespread phenomenon at the papal court and among the city's rich and noble families – the Della Valle, the Cesi, Sassi, Farnese – were practically competing to corner the market as it were.

Sponsor of an ambitious cultural policy, Julius II undertook grandiose projects such as the rebuilding of Saint Peter's Basilica, under the direction of Donato Bramante. The pope wanted to place the huge tomb by Michelangelo inside the new basilica. The first design, agreed upon with the pope in 1505, called for a rectangular structure, with three orders that diminished going upward, with fourty statues. Michelangelo went to Carrara to choose the marble he needed and returned with it early in 1506. But he was very disappointed when he had to wait endlessly for an audience with the pope who was already bored with the project. In the end, the exasperated artist sent word to His Holiness saying that if he wanted to see him, he would have to come in person, and having said that he fled to Florence. "You cannot work with him," said Julius – who was just as domineering and irascible – complaining of Michelangelo's difficult character; he behaved as no other artist would have dared and even risked causing a diplomatic incident between Rome and Florence. In fact, it took three Papal Briefs to the Florentine authorities to convince the sculptor to retreat from his position and agree to meet the pope and ask his pardon. The two finally made peace with each other in Bologna in November of that same year: Julius, had in the interim entered the city and triumphantly defeated the Bentivoglio rule. To seal the peace between patron and artist, the pope asked Michelangelo to make a bronze portrait of him to place in a niche on the façade of Saint Petronius. That statue was destroyed five years later when the Bentivoglio retook the city.

This was how the tormented design and construction of the Monument to Julius II ("the tragedy of the burial," as Michelangelo defined it) began. It would be marked by six different contracts and was only completed in 1545 when the monument was finally placed in San Pietro in Vincoli. In 1508 the pope ordered two extraordinarily important decorations and commissioned Raphael and Michelangelo respectively. Both artists moved to Rome for the purpose. While Raphael was decorating the new pontifical apartment in the Vatican Palace, with frescoes of the *School of Athens* and the *Liberation of Saint Peter,* Michelangelo was frescoing the ceiling of the Sistine Chapel. He had reluctantly accepted the job that was offered to him as the result of ruthless court intrigues. According to the biographers it was Bramante and other courtiers who urged the pope to assign the Florentine artist such a huge and difficult task because they were convinced that if Buonarroti accepted he would prove to be a lesser artist than Raphael. Michelangelo worked indefatigably and completely alone in a position that tortured his body; he considered the task a challenge to himself and tradition. After four years of unceasing work the ceiling was unveiled in its entirety in 1512 with the story of humanity *ante legem* with the *Seers* and the *Ancestors of Christ*. When Julius II suggested that the artist add some touches of gold, saying that otherwise the painting would be "poor," Michelangelo resolutely replied "Those who are painted here [...] were poor too" (Condivi).

The pope died shortly thereafter, in 1513, and Michelangelo signed a new contract with his heirs for a funeral monument, that was smaller and had fewer statues than the earlier design. The two *Slaves* – now in the Louvre – and the *Moses* which was used in the end were planned for the new version.

In Florence for Leo X. The new Pope Leo X, who was born Giovanni de' Medici, son of Lorenzo the Magnificent, relieved Michelangelo of having to complete his predecessor's tomb and asked him to return to Florence to work on the Medici buildings: Palazzo Medici, the San Lorenzo complex, and the villa at Poggio a Caiano. The Medici family had returned to Florence just one year before (1512), repossessed its property and control of the government bringing an end to the long Repub-

On page 75,
Raphael,
Leo X with Two Cardinals,
1516-1518;
Florence, Uffizi.

Basilica
of San Lorenzo,
Florence.

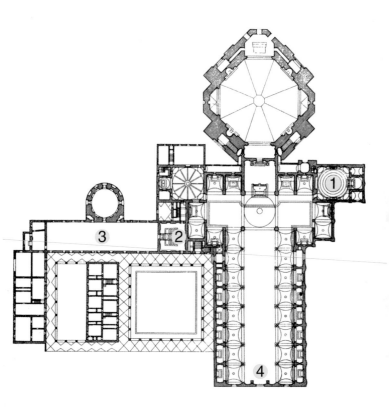

Plan of the Basilica
of San Lorenzo, Florence:
1. New Sacristy
2. Laurentian Library, Vestibule
3. Laurentian Library, Reading Room
4. Tribune of the Relics

lican interlude. The cultural policies of Pope Leo X in Florence aimed at emphasizing the return of the Medici and reaffirming the family's prestige.

After a competition called between 1515 and 1516 Leo X appointed Michelangelo to design the façade for San Lorenzo, the Medici family church built to plans by Brunelleschi nearly one hundred years before. Buonarroti immediately set to work, drawing plans and building models and even went to Pietrasanta to select the marble. But on 10 March 1520 the pope relieved him of

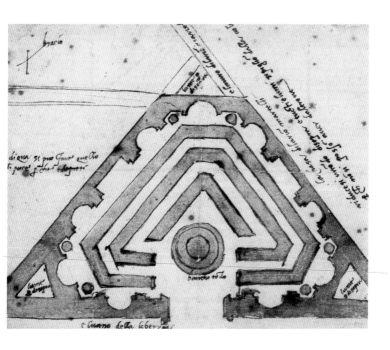

"Third Design"
for the Façade of San Lorenzo,
1517; Florence,
Casa Buonarroti.

Design for a room of rare
books in the Laurentian
Library, 1525; Florence,
Casa Buonarroti.

the assignment and the façade was never built, in spite of the artist's disappointment. However, the interior, with the balcony to display reliquaries was completed to Buonarroti's plans.

While he was working on San Lorenzo, on request of Leo X Michelangelo designed the "kneeling" windows which in 1517 enclosed the public loggia at the corner of the Palazzo Medici. Still for the Laurentian complex, via the offices of Cardinal Giulio de' Medici, in 1519 the pope asked Michelangelo to build the New Sacristy next to the right transept of the church. To fulfill his father's wishes the pope wanted to build a memorial chapel to house the tombs of Lorenzo the Magnificent and his brother, Giuliano, along with those of Giuliano Duke of Nemours and Lorenzo, Duke of Urbino, namesakes, brother and nephew of Leo X, who had died in 1516 and 1519, respectively. Michelangelo began the work in 1520 and carried on with interruptions and delays until 1534 when he stopped and departed for Rome, for the last time. The New Sacristy, one of Michelangelo's greatest achievements, became the prototype for Florentine Mannerist architecture. Generations of artists have gone there to study and copy the sculptures of *Dawn, Dusk, Day* and *Night* on the tombs. They are the ultimate renderings of the human form, its variety of poses, its grief and heroism as it faces time "that consumes everything" (Condivi).

In the meantime, in 1521 the sculptor sent the second version of the marble *Christ Bearing the Cross* to Rome for the church of Santa Maria Sopra Minerva. The first ver-

On page 81,
The Risen Christ,
1514-1516;
Bassano Romano,
Church of San Vincenzo
Martire, sacristy.

Madonna and Child,
c. 1525; Florence, Casa
Buonarroti. The theme
of the *Madonna lactans*
appears in the *Virgin and
Child* in the New Sacristy.

sion that had been commissioned by the Roman noble-man, Metello Vari, in 1514 has recently been recognized as the statue in the sacristy of San Vincenzo Martire at Bassano Romano.

Leo X died on 1 December 1521 and his successor, Hadrian VI reigned for a very short time. On 18 November 1523 Cardinal Giulio de' Medici became Pope Clement VII. While he was monitoring the plans and work for the New Sacristy, in 1523 the new Medici pope asked Michelangelo to build a library to house the family's huge collection of books and manuscripts inside the Laurentian complex. The pope picked up the old plans of Lorenzo the Magnificent who, as we have seen, had set up a sort of stonecutter's yard in the garden of San Marco. Michelangelo developed the plans for the Laurentian Library: the architecture of the two rooms, vestibule and reading room, the stairs, the inlaid *cotto* floor, the wooden ceiling and wooden desks. He departed for Rome in 1534, leaving yet another project unfinished; it was completed about forty years later under Cosimo I.

The Sack of Rome and the Republic in Florence. The Medici projects that Michelangelo was working on in Florence came to a sudden halt in 1527 during a second uprising that once again led to Medici's loss of power and the reestablishment of a Savonarola-inspired republic. This revolt was encouraged by the Sack of Rome five days earlier: on 16 May the troops of the Emperor Charles V invaded Rome and endangered even the life of Pope Clement VII himself. In Florence, the gonfalonier Niccolò Capponi commissioned Michelangelo, who supported the new government, to carve a gigantic marble statue of *Hercules and Cacus* to place near the *David* in front of the Palazzo della Signoria. The sculpture was later made for the Medici by Baccio Bandinelli. In the meantime, the economic crisis was compounded by the plague that decimated the population and even took away the artist's younger brother, Buonarroto.

After the humiliation of the Sack of Rome, the Medici pope reached an agreement with Charles V, promising to crown him emperor in exchange for support in restoring his family to the government of Florence. Early in 1529 the news reached Florence that the pope was preparing to besiege the city with the help of the imperial troops. On 6 April Michelangelo, who had already joined the Com-

*Studies for the head
of Leda,*
c. 1530; Florence,
Casa Buonarroti.

mittee of Nine of the Florentine Militia, was appointed governor and procurator general of the fortifications with the task of reinforcing and completing the defensive system, especially along the hill of San Miniato. In order to carry out this task to the best, in July he went to Ferrara to study the excellent Estensi fortifications. On that occasion Alfonso I d'Este asked the artist to paint a *Leda and the Swan*. D'Este never received the painting; the artist gave it to Antonio Mini along with some drawings and the preparatory cartoon; the Leda ended up in France where it was destroyed at the end of the XVII century. In the meantime, the June 1529 Treaty of Barcelona sanctioned the alliance between Charles V and Clement VII. Perhaps seeing the criticality of the situation, Michelangelo fled towards France and the court of Francis I. He was declared a rebel by the City of Florence with the threat of having all his assets confiscated, however, he was promised a pardon if he returned immediately. Buonarroti interrupted his journey at Venice and under some pressure, returned to Florence in November, with the only penalty that the Great Council barred him for three years. While in Florence that was under siege, Michelangelo resumed his work on the fortifications and ordered the bell tower of San Miniato covered with wool

Opposite page, above,
*Studies for the fortifications
of Porta al Prato d'Ognissanti*, 1527;
Florence, Casa Buonarroti.

Below,
*Plan for a bastion
for a city gate*,
1527; Florence,
Casa Buonarroti.

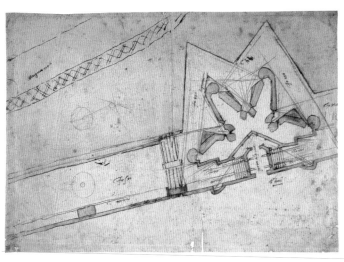

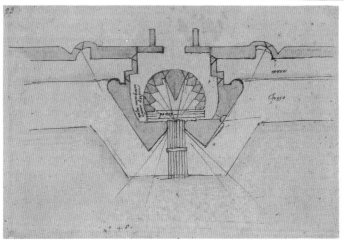

87

mattresses to protect it from artillery fire. The Medici were restored to power after Florence was forced to surrender in August 1530. Michelangelo was pardoned once again thanks to the intervention of Clement VII who wanted him to complete the Medici tombs. During this same period the artist carved the *David-Apollo* (Museo del Bargello) for Baccio Valori, the new governor. And, he went back to work on the Monument to Julius II under a new contract signed in 1532 that called for a wall monument in San Pietro in Vincoli. During the two years from 1532-34 the artist divided his time between Florence and Rome. He also prepared cartoons that were later given to Portormo or Sebastiano del Piombo for paintings (*Resurrection of Lazarus, Noli me Tangere* and *Venus and Cupid*). However, notwithstanding the protection of Pope Clement VII, Alessandro de' Medici who had become Duke of Tuscany, could not bring himself to pardon the artist who had refused to design a fortress to "protect" the Florentines. The complex, the Fortezza di San Giovanni, known as "da Basso," was built instead by Antonio da Sangallo the Younger. Thus, perhaps because of the despotism of Alessandro de' Medici, or because of his father's death, or even because of his friendship with Tommaso Cavalieri whom he had met two years before – Michelangelo left Florence forever, and moved to Rome in 1534. He left the sites of San Lorenzo, the New Sacristy and the Laurentian Library open and unfinished. In his studio in Via Mozza (now Via San Zanobi) he left wax and terracotta models, cartoons and drawings, the four *Slaves* (in

Pontormo (?), *Noli Me Tangere*
(to a cartoon by Michelangelo),
c. 1532; Florence, Casa Buonarroti.

the Galleria dell'Accademia), the *Victory* (Palazzo Vecchio museum), as well as the marble statues carved for the Monument to Julius II that were never used.

In 1537, Alessandro was assassinated by his cousin Lorenzino whom Michelangelo would later immortalize in the marble bust of *Brutus* he carved for Cardinal Ridolfi, an exiled Florentine. Cosimo I was now Duke of Tuscany; with clarity of mind and determination he built and ruled a modern state. During his government Cosimo invited Michelangelo to return to the city, but it was in vain. Therefore, he had to concern himself personally with completing the work on the San Lorenzo complex using the services of his outstanding court artists such as Giorgio Vasari and Bartolomeo Ammannati, but he never had the satisfaction of bringing Florence's greatest artist home.

Rome. In 1534 Michelangelo who was at the peak of his fame, with his greatness acknowledged by contemporary artists, settled in the papal city where he would remain for thirty years until his death. If it is clear that with the Sack of Rome in 1527 the dream of a restoration of a Rome as *caput mundi* pursued by the bellicose Julius II and the two Medici popes (Leo X and Clement XII) was definitively shattered on the political level – proving that Italy and her little states were merely pawns in the large-scale conflict among the great foreign powers – it is just as true that the tendencies that had shifted the center of Renaissance culture from Florence to Rome early in the XVI century continued to allow the Urbe to maintain its

Titian,
Portrait of Pietro Aretino,
1545; Florence,
Galleria Palatina.

Étienne Delaune,
Leda, after
Michelangelo,
c. 1545; Florence,
Gabinetto Disegni
e Stampe degli Uffizi.

S

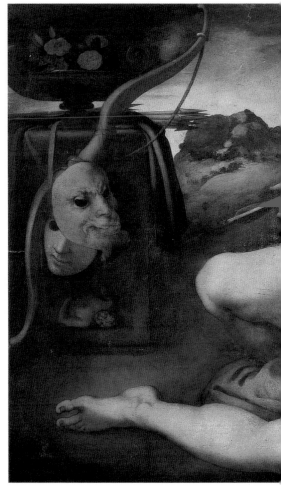

Pontormo, *Venus and Cupid* (after a cartoon by Michelangelo), c. 1533; Florence, Galleria dell'Accademia. Commissioned by Bartolomeo Bettini for his palazzo, the painting was flanked by portraits of Tuscan poets by Agnolo Bronzino.

Michelangelo, study
for the *Last Judgment*,
1533-1534; Florence,
Casa Buonarroti.

Giulio Clovio, copy of Michelangelo's *Last Judgment*,
second half of the XVI century; Florence, Casa Buonarroti.
This copy is important because
it was painted before Daniele da Volterra
was ordered to cover the nudes in 1564.

cultural primacy throughout Europe. When Michelangelo returned to the city Clement VII had been dead for a short time. His successor was Cardinal Alessandro Farnese who took the name of Paul III: he was one of the era's most refined collectors and greatest men of culture. Indeed, his large collection of ancient statuary included pieces such as the *Herucles* and the *Bull* which are both known as *Farnese*.

Paul III entrusted Michelangelo with a task that had already been planned by Clement VII: a continuation of the decorations of the Sistine Chapel that had begun with the ceiling frescoes and was to be completed with a grandiose *Last Judgment* on the wall behind the altar to replace Perugino's *Assumption of the Virgin*. So, in 1536, after twenty-four years the artist was back in the Sistine chapel. He proposed a different vision, animated by dramatic, apocalyptic accents, reflected in a whirl of ceaseless motion suspended in the air. When he had completed this artistic feat, once again the pope relieved him of the obligation to work on the Monument to Julius II. In 1542, barely one year after the *Last Judgment* Paul III wanted Buonarroti to decorate the Pauline Chapel that had recently been built by Antonio da Sangallo. The artist transferred his personal spiritual wounds to the frescoes portraying the *Conversion of Saint Paul* and the *Crucifixion of Saint Peter*. Michelangelo's religious and philosophical meditations were also revealed in the poems and drawings he gave to Vittoria Colonna, a poetess close to the reformed Catholic milieus, whom the

artist considered his spiritual guide. She was the muse with whom he could correspond in writing and engage in learned conversations. Michelangelo's works – painting, sculpture, and writings – were an expression of the grim and restless climate pervading the Church that had to deal with the new religious ferment, pressed by the urgent need to give a strong and decisive response to the Lutheran Reformation. Among the first steps in the Catholic counteroffensive were the reopening of the Holy Inquisition in 1542 and the Council of Trent in 1545 which led to the Counterreformation.

During the 1540s Michelangelo was laden with work, projects of huge magnitude. He had the seemingly endless undertaking of the Monument to Julius II (completed in 1545) and new assignments as architect to the Pope: the piazzale of the Capitoline Hill, the remodeling of the palazzo where the pope's family dwelt and, above all he continued with the work on Saint Peter's as he had been appointed chief architect of the *Fabbrica di San Pietro* in 1546. His appointment was confirmed by Paul III's successors and he had to work without pay until his death because (as the contract reads) "he served the *fabrica* out of

On page 99,
Daniele da Volterra (head)
and Giambologna (bust)
Bust of Michelangelo,
1564-1566 (head),
c. 1570 (bust);
Florence, Casa Buonarroti.

Francesco Vinea,
*Michelangelo Reciting
his Poems to Vittoria Colonna*,
c. 1865; Florence,
Palazzo Pitti,
Monumental apartments.

love of God." Basically for Julius III and Paul IV his work consisted mainly of supplying plans and supervision.

In the last part of his life Michelangelo devoted himself mainly to architecture, but early in the 1550s he took up carving again and returned to the theme of the *Pietà* with the intention of making a statue for his own tomb.

He began work on the *Pietà* (now in the Museo dell'Opera del Duomo in Florence) when he was around seventy. It was close to completion in 1555 but the marble broke, so he stopped, however, it was purchased by Francesco Bandini. The *Palestrina Pietà*, which may have been done by the artist's close followers, reflects Michelangelo's considerations on this theme. During the same period he worked on another version of the same theme in the *Rondandini Pietà,* the statue he was working on when he died.

The Last Return to Florence. Michelangelo died in Rome on 18 February 1564 shortly before his eighty-ninth birthday; he expired in the home of Macel de' Corvi near Trajan's Forum. Around him were his dearest friends, including Tommaso de' Cavalieri and Daniele da Volterra. Just one month before, the Council of Trent ordered that the nude figures in the *Last Judgment* be covered, and it was Daniele da Volterra who would do it.

Pupil of Michelangelo (?),
Palestrina Pietà,
c. 1555; Florence,
Galleria dell'Accademia.

On 11 March Leonardo Buonarroti, the artist's nephew secretly brought his uncle's remains back to Florence. Funeral services, ordered by Cosimo I de' Medici, were held in San Lorenzo on 14 July. The grandiose displays and decorations were made by the artists from the Accademia delle Arti del Disegno under the guidance of Giorgio Vasari. The academy had been established the year before under the direction of the Medici duke and the aegis of Buonarroti himself. Benedetto Varchi, renowned man of letters, gave the funeral oration.

Giorgio Vasari designed the funeral monument, following the suggestions of Don Vincenzo Borghini, with a concept that brought together Michelangelo's arts, architecture, sculpture and painting, in the allegorical marble figures seated at the edges of the pedestal. The tomb was erected in the Basilica of Santa Croce (1578) near the Buonarroti homes. The church already housed the remains of important public figures and it was where Michelangelo's father himself was buried. To build the monument Leonardo Buonarroti donated the unused marbles that were still in the atelier on Via Mozza and he gave the four *Slaves* and the *Victory* to Cosimo I.

The myth of Michelangelo had already been born, it had been shaped by the artist himself and through his contemporary biographers Condivi and Vasari, disseminated by Benedetto Varchi's lessons at the Accademia Fiorentina and fueled by the cultural policies pursued by Cosimo I de' Medici. The echoes of the myth would go beyond the biography of the artist starting with the second edi-

tion of the *Lives of the Painters, Sculptors and Architects* published by Giorgio Vasari in 1568 in which Michelangelo's life seems to represent the zenith of artistic development. It is a myth that has been expanded, and modified over the centuries and it has continuously left its mark even with self-criticism. Here we can barely touch on it to suggest its scope, offering a bird's eye view of some of its significant stages. It began in Florence and spans the world: the Medici collections, the XVII century paintings in Casa Buonarroti with scenes from the artist's life, the Tribune built in the Galleria dell'Accademia to host the *David* (1872), the four-hundredth centennial celebrations in 1875, the multitude of copies of his works, XX century literature and films that turned his life into a historical novel, a still unexhausted harvest of bibliography, epoch-making restorations and exhibitions that draw the world's attention.

All of this contributes to presenting Michelangelo, even today, as the most famous artist of all times: a man whose personality is conveyed by his works and writings that had always been deemed complex and grandiose, in some ways fleeting and always, incredibly current.

EXIMIIS AR
TIBVS BONAR
ROTAM AD CÆ
LV HAVD EVE
CTV CREDAS
ILLAS POTIVS
DIVINO IPSIVS
INGENIO EX
CVLTAS EO
SECVM ELATAS
EXISTIMA

On page 105,
Giorgio Vasari,
Michelangelo's Tomb,
1570; Florence,
Basilica of Santa Croce.

Sigismondo Coccapani,
The Four Arts Crowning Michelangelo,
c. 1612-1628; Florence,
Casa Buonarroti.

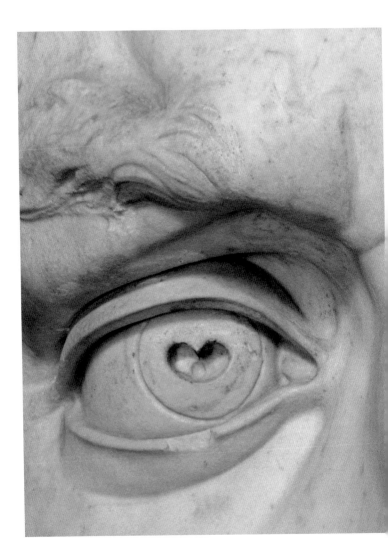

Sculpture

In a letter to the Florentine historian and philologist, Benedetto Varchi, Michelangelo wrote: "For me sculpture is what you do by removing"; and he added, in the same letter, that the other sculpture "that you do by adding, is similar to painting." Therefore, for Buonarroti sculpting meant taking hammer and chisel to the marble and removing the superfluous, and not shaping a malleable material. Other important insights into what sculpture meant to the artist come from some of his poems that say "*The best of artists hath no thought to show / Which the rough stone in its superfluous shell / Doth not include*": So, by striking the side of a piece of marble, the sculptor struggles to bring the secrets out of the hard material. Michelangelo's approach was clearly influenced by Neo-Platonic thought: the idea, the shape of the statue is already inside the marble, the chisel sets it free, the manual work is at the service of a spiritual revelation. Indeed, that same concept is expressed in a passage by the V century Christian philosopher Pseudo-Dionysus the Areopagite, to whom several Neoplatonic texts are indebted: "The art of sculpting an image in stone that seems alive," he wrote, "is done by removing all that prevents a clear view of the latent shape, revealing its hidden beauty by removing only the superfluous."

THE MADONNA OF THE STAIRS

This relief carving is the earliest of Michelangelo's surviving sculptures. It dates from around 1490, when he was frequenting the sculpture garden of San Marco where, while studying ancient statues he had the opportunity of admiring Donatello's works thanks to the guidance offered by Bertoldo di Giovanni who was conservator of the Medici "garden" and one of the last generation of the great Florentine master's pupils.

In the *Madonna of the Stairs* Michelangelo experimented with Donatello's *stiacciato*, flattened, technique. This consisted of creating a sense of depth and three-dimensionality by barely carving the figures, so they were almost flattened against the surface, gradually diminishing in thickness towards the background. The use of this technique and the iconography reveal that Michelangelo had studied Donatello's statues such as the *Pazzi Madonna* (c. 1442; Berlin, Staatliche Museen Prussicher Kulturbesitz) or the *Del Pugliese-Dudley Madonna* (c. 1440; London, Victoria and Albert Museum).

The first to note Donatello's influence on Michelangelo's bas-relief that is dated around 1490, was Giorgio Vasari in the second edition of *Lives* (1568). Vasari was also the first to mention this piece that Michelangelo's nephew, Leonardo Buonarroti had given to Cosimo I de' Medici, Grand Duke of Tuscany. The biographer from Arezzo writes of "… a Madonna of marble in low-relief by the hand of Michelangelo, little more than one *braccio* in

Madonna of the Stairs,
c. 1490,
marble, 57.1 x 40.5 cm;
Florence, Casa Buonarroti.

Page 108,
David, detail,
1501-1504; Florence,
Galleria dell'Accademia.

height, in which when a lad, at this same time, wishing to counterfeit the manner of Donatello, he acquitted himself so well that it seems as if by Donatello's hand..." Compared with Donatello's *Madonnas* Michelangelo's relief has other compositional elements. In the Buonarroti carving the Virgin Mary does not look tenderly at the Child, but appears to be absorbed in thought about the destiny of her sleeping Son. He is portrayed from the back, an unusual iconographic choice. Furthermore, the musculature is powerful, not like a child's and perhaps was influenced by the ancient *Farnese Hercules.* And finally, Jesus has his right arm behind His back, while His lower torso and head are turned in opposite directions with a solution that Michelangelo would later use in the statue of *Day* in the New Sacristy. The monumental profile of Mary embracing her powerful Son stands out against the stairs in the background with the clear symbolism of the Virgin herself as the *scala coeli.* The stairs have also been interpreted as Marsilio Ficino' s theory of the five levels of being (five stairs in Michelangelo's statue) and his stair of love that joins the earthly to the divine. There is a definite parallel in a 1495 composition by Domenico Benivieni, a friend of Ficino, who in the *Scala della vita spirituale sopra il nome di Maria* compares the five letters of her name to the five steps of a staircase.

Unruly children are scampering at the top of the stairs. One of them is handing a piece of cloth to another, perhaps an allusion to the Shroud of the Passion which is probably the central theme of the entire composition.

THE BATTLE OF THE CENTAURS

According to Vasari, Michelangelo himself gave the *Battle of the Centaurs* which he carved between 1490 and 1492 to Lorenzo the Magnificent. Condivi, on the other hand, who considers it a piece completed after Lorenzo's death in April 1492, does not clarify whether the unfinished look was a deliberate choice on the part of the artist or he merely stopped working on it when Lorenzo died; upset by the loss, Michelangelo left the Medici palace and returned to his father's home. However, it has recently been confirmed that the artist may have gone back to work on the marble even after 1494 and for about a decade. This hypothesis is based on the several *pentimenti* and the fact that some of the figures are similar to the *Pitti Tondo* from 1504-1505 (Florence, Museo Nazionale del Bargello; see pages 208-213).

The subject, the battle between the Lapithae and Centaurs – is based on texts by Hyginus and Ovid and had already been treated by other Florentine artists such as Bartolomeo di Giovanni and Piero di Cosimo. Condivi maintains that it was Agnolo Poliziano, the outstanding figure in Lorenzo's milieu, who suggested the classical theme to the young sculptor as it reflected the taste for antiquities that pervaded the Medici cultural environment. According to a Neo-Platonic interpretation, the relief portrays a *psycomachia*, a battle between the animal and spiritual components of the human soul.

Battle of the Centaurs,
1490-1492,
marble, 80 x 90.5 cm;
Florence, Casa Buonarroti.

From the iconographic standpoint Michelangelo probably drew his generic inspiration from earlier works such as the *Battle of the Nudes* by Antonio Pollaiolo that was portrayed in several engravings and Bertoldo's bronze relief of the *Battle* (Florence, Museo Nazionale del Bargello) which, in turn, was based on the front of an ancient Roman sarcophagus in the Camposanto in Pisa. However, Michelangelo's statue already presents a highly personal imprint and mature workmanship which recalls a model selected by the young, nonconformist genius and completely independently, that is Giovanni Pisano's pulpit in the Pisa Baptistry. The sculptural technique and the marked degree of finishing on the more visible parts to the detriment of the lower sections that remained rougher also recall that powerful XIV century carving.

In general, the theme, that Condivi calls the *Rape of Deianira and Battle of the Centaurs,* seems mainly to offer the artist the inspiration for an exhaustive study of nudes. The tangled mass of bodies, in every possible position, could not but offer the artist an endless repertory that he could use throughout his life. Due to the undefined background, and lack of a frame, the *Battle of the Centaurs* may well be considered Michelangelo's first "unfinished" sculpture.

Santo Spirito Crucifix

After Lorenzo the Magnificent's death (1492) Michelangelo received permission from the prior of Santo Spirit, Niccolò di Giovanni di Lapo Bicchiellini, to take bodies buried in the Augustinian complex and "flay" them to study anatomy. Out of gratitude Michelangelo carved a "… a Crucifix of wood, which was placed […] above the lunette of the high-altar; doing this to please the Prior, who placed rooms at his disposal" (Vasari, 1568).

This sculpture, which in the XVII century was moved from the main altar to other rooms and then forgotten, was found within the monastery and identified as Michelangelo's *Crucifix* in the 1960s. Now it is displayed in the sacristy (Lisner 1962 and ff.). This identification, that had been contested in the past, is now accepted by the majority of today's critics and scholars. Therefore, it is datable between April 1492 and October 1494, that is the period between Lorenzo's death and Michelangelo's escape from Florence a few weeks before the Medicis were banished.

The figure of Christ is based on precise anatomical knowledge. The typology of the Crucifix – which is interesting to compare with Donatello's wooden Crucifix in Santa Croce – seems to have been influenced by the sermons of Savonarola who urged emphasis on the defenseless, delicate and fragile aspect of Christ to make Him appear even more vulnerable.

Crucifix,
1492-1494,
polychrome wood, 139 x 135 cm;
Florence, Santo Spirito.

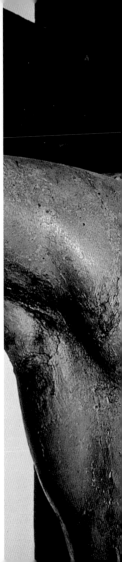

SCULPTURES FOR THE TOMB OF SAINT DOMINIC: ANGEL HOLDING A CANDELABRUM, SAINT PROCOLUS, SAINT PETRONIUS

In the autumn of 1494, fear, uncertainty and tension filled the air throughout Florence where the people were afraid of the arrival of the French army led by King Charles VIII and where the Dominican monk Girolamo Savonarola was gaining influence to the detriment of Piero de' Medici who, along with his family was exiled in November by the newly formed, post-insurrection republican government. Given those circumstances, in October Michelangelo decided to leave Florence and go first to Venice and then to Bologna. There he was the guest of Gianfrancesco Aldrovandi, an educated nobleman who also had an excellent relationship with the Medicis. It was thanks to him that Michelangelo, who did not belong to any sculptural workshop, and never registered with any guild, could obtain an important commission: three statues for the Tomb of Saint Dominic, in the church dedicated to the saint – and one of the city's most important churches.

The monument had been begun by Nicola Pisano and his helpers in the XIV century; then between 1469 and 1473 Niccolò dell'Arca had worked on the pinnacle and crowing, but never completed them. Michelangelo had to carve three moderate-sized marble figures to fit into a setting designed by others: an *Angel Holding a Cande-*

Angel Holding a Candelabrum,
1494-1495,
marble, height 51.5 cm;
Bologna, San Domenico, Tomb of Saint Dominic.

Saint Petronius,
1494-1495,
marble, height 58.5 cm;
Bologna, San Domenico, Tomb of Saint Dominic.

labrum, Saint Petronius bishop and patron saint of Bologna, and *Saint Procolus,* a Roman soldier who converted to Christianity and was subsequently martyred.

The *Angel* is both impressive and monumental, these features are further offset by the comparison with its companion pieces, the graceful *Angel* by Niccolò d'Arca. Here, what would become one of the most admired features of Michelangelo's art is already evident, that is his ability to dress his statues with draping which rather than hiding, enhances the body; in this sense, too, a comparison with the older angel is quite enlightening. The face, the hair created with a drill, and mainly the treatment of the overly soft hands, lacking any bone structure, echo features of Nicola Pisano's statues on the same tomb, as if Michelangelo had wanted to duplicate – or counterfeit – the XIV century master's works.

Saint Procolus,
1494-1495,
marble, height 64 cm;
Bologna, San Domenico, Tomb of Saint Dominic.

The *Saint Petronius* was probably carved from a piece of marble already roughed by Niccolò dell'Arca. The figure holds a scale model of the city of Bologna in his hand where we can recognize the Garisenda and Asinelli towers. The draping with its swirling folds and deep recesses reflects the influence of Jacopo della Quercia an early XV century Sienese artist and author of the grandiose central door of San Petronio in Bologna.

The figure of *Saint Proculus* is so different that it is hard to believe that the two statues are contemporary with each other. The saint is heroic and permeated with an inner tension that is revealed by the knitted brow, the proud, bold and dynamic pose, and the tight hands which compared to those of the *Angel* reveal enormous expressive power. Michelangelo must certainly have known Francesco del Cossa's allegorical fresco of the month of *March* in the Schifanoia palace in Ferrara: the relationship with the *Saint Proculus* is undeniable. Michelangelo's statue was irreparably damaged by a fall in 1572; the metal lance it originally held in its hand has since been lost.

BACCHUS

In Rome, while he was living and working in the home of the banker Jacopo Galli, Michelangelo carved the *Bacchus* for Cardinal Raffaele Sansoni Riario, a client of Galli's bank. The prelate ordered the statue in 1496 and wanted it for the grandiose palace he was building, the Palazzo della Cancelleria, surrounded by the countless pieces in his collection of antiquities – one of the most prestigious in all Rome. It was to the Cardinal that Michelangelo had sold his *Sleeping Cupid* passing it off as an archeological find (see page 46). And even though he had discovered the fraud, the cardinal wanted to meet the Florentine counterfeiter who, if nothing else, had proved to have a great talent and to be an unequaled imitator of antiquities. According to the patron's intentions, the *Bacchus* was to have competed with his classical pieces. But when the cardinal saw the statue, he rejected it and left it in Galli's home.

In a drawing by the Dutch painter, Maarten van Heemskerck (between 1532 and 1535) the life-sized *Bacchus* stands out as the greatest piece among the many antiques and curiosities scattered throughout Galli's Rome garden (Berlin, Staatliche Museen Preussicher Kulturbesitz, inv. n. 79 D 2, fol. 72r; see pages 50-52). As the drawing shows, the statue had been damaged in the meantime and the right wrist was broken; the hand and goblet were later reattached and repaired.

Bacchus,
1496-1497,
marble, height 209 cm;
Florence, Museo Nazionale del Bargello.

To create such a totally unique and original figure Michelangelo had taken inspirational points from antiquity. Even his contemporaries such as Vasari (1550; 1568) had noted a certain a certain ambiguity in the statue to which the artist had given the "youthful slenderness of the male and the fullness and roundness of the female." The figure, with all the traditional attributes of the god (the crown of vine leaves, the goblet, the bunch of grapes, the feline animal skin) is not in the traditional, classically balanced pose. Rather he is swaying and off balance, with his back arched, belly protruding and evidently drunk. It is certainly an unusual iconography which may have been the cause of the cardinal's disappointment. Among the many ancient statues of Bacchus there is not a single one portraying him in such an unstable equilibrium; however, in relief carvings the god is sometimes depicted as supported by the members of his entourage.

Among the classical statues that may have inspired Michelangelo, the most likely model could be the gigantic portrait-statue of *Antinoos* – favorite of the emperor Hadrian – with the attributes of Bacchus, a statue which in the XVI century was part of the Farnese collection and is now in the Museo Archeologico in Naples. However, the *Antinoos* does not have the young satyr who is slyly eating from the grapes in the god's hand. In Michelangelo's statue, the little thief, half-wild animal twists on himself behind the legs of Bacchus and becomes an expedient to invite the viewer to go around the group which, from any viewpoint is in perfect equilibrium, and discover new details. The facial expression (which is ruined by two veins in the marble itself) with the half-open mouth and eyes turned upward reveals an interest in Hellenistic sculpture and its sentimental notes.

In 1572 Francesco I de' Medici purchased the *Bacchus* from Galli for 280 *scudi* and had it placed in the Uffizi, in a corridor next to an ancient *Bacchus* to prove the great superiority of the modern statue.

YOUNG ARCHER

There is another life-sized marble statue by Michelangelo that comes from the house of Jacopo Galli in Rome. It has been defined as an *Apollo* or *Cupid*. The XVI century scholar, Ulisse Adrovandi (1556), mentioned two important details: there was a vase at its feet, an unusual attribute for either of the two gods, and he was wingless. Thanks to recent studies, mainly by Kathleen Weil-Garris Brandt (1996, 1997 and after) and James Draper (1997) we have the hypothesis that the statue could be the *Young Archer* now in the Whitney Mansion owned by the Services Culturels of the French Embassy in New York. Early in the XX century it had been in the hands of the great Florentine antiquarian Stefano Bardini who had attributed it to Michelangelo. However, for many years that attribution was only accepted by Alessandro Parronchi (1968) even though he had never seen the original. During the XVII century the statue of the slender youth with a quiver on his shoulder, now severely damaged by time, stood in an outdoor niche on the façade of Villa Borghese in Rome. During the following century the French artist Jean-Robert Ango (New York, Smithsonian Institution, Cooper-Hewitt, National Design Museum, inv. n. 1997-110-1-4) saw and drew it. Its placement in a famous collection is more than a secondary part of the statue's historical context. Ango's drawings show that the figure – which was still intact – rotated on itself in an unusual pose, in the act of taking an arrow

Young Archer,
c. 1496-1497,
marble, height 100 cm (without base);
New York, Services Culturels de l'Ambassade de France.

from the quiver, with his right arm raised and back, and his left leg was supported by a vase.

Even if there are still uncertainties, the *Young Archer* could be from Michelangelo's youthful period for more than one reason. One of these was his proximity to Bertoldo which had induced Hirst (1996) to attribute it to him. The subdued but throbbing vitality in the twisting torso, with effects similar to the Santo Spirito *Crucifix*; the full face and compact curls that strongly resemble the angels in the *Manchester Madonna*, and the marble angel in Bologna; and the "unfinished" effect on some parts (not to be confused with abrasions caused by the elements) which, juxtaposed with the finish on other parts, reveals an expressive and technical phase compatible with the Galli *Bacchus* that would have been made slightly earlier, all point to Michelangelo's autography.

THE VATICAN PIETÀ

The *Pietà* in Saint Peter's Basilica in the Vatican was Michelangelo's first important Roman commission. It is also the only piece he ever signed: engraved in the band diagonally crossing the Virgin's torso are the words MICHELANGELUS BONAROTUS FLORENT[INUS] FACIEBAT. The famous marble group was ordered by the French cardinal Jean Bilhères de Lagraulas, ambassador of King Charles VIII of France to Pope Alexander VI, who stipulated the contract in 1498 via the banker Jacopo Galli, who was friend to both Michelangelo and the cardinal.

Originally the *Pietà* was destined for the cardinal's tomb in Santa Petronilla, an early Christian chapel annexed to the Constantinian Basilica that had been demolished in order to build the new Saint Peter's where Michelangelo's masterpiece would later stand. Regarding the Christ Vasari wrote (1568): "... nor let anyone think to see greater beauty of members or more mastery of art in a body or a nude with more detail in the muscles, veins and nerves over the framework of the bones, nor yet a corpse more similar than this to a real corpse. Here is the perfect sweetness in the expression of the head, harmony in the joints and attachments of the arms, legs, and trunk, and the pulses and veins so wrought, that in truth Wonder herself must marvel that the hand of a craftsman should have been able to execute so divinely and so perfectly, in so short a time, a work so admirable.." And here is how the artist's famous biographer, Condivi (1553) described

Pietà,
1498-1499,
marble, height 174 cm;
Vatican City, Saint Peter's Basilica.

the figure of the Virgin: "Seated on a rock where the cross had stood, with her dead Son on her lap, of such rare beauty that no person who looks… within… cannot be moved." Already, these few words reveal the main features of this marvelous statue. On the one hand is the sculptor's skill, the virtuoso technique that dwelt on the meticulous rendering of the anatomical details; and on the other the composed beauty of the figures, especially the delicate and very young Virgin Mary – the touching poetry of a group which is so highly polished that it gleams like alabaster rather than marble. Never again would this master of the "unfinished" create such a clean, complete statue that seems to have been carved to prove the attainment of a formal milestone that he would then leave behind as he moved forward.

To demonstrate his skill even further, Michelangelo carved the *Pietà* from a single block of marble without adding any pieces. He himself selected the marble at the Carrara quarries and traveled with it back to Rome, a journey that lasted nine months. In Michelangelo's masterpiece Mary, absorbed in grief, contemplates her dead Son who had been taken down from the cross; she supports Him with her right hand, but only touches the divine body through the shroud, and holds her left hand open in a gesture that seems to introduce the observer to the tragedy and mystery of the Redeemer's sacrifice. From the compositional standpoint the statue creates a perfect balance between the two only apparently contrasting shapes: on the one hand is the seated, erect figure

of the Virgin, on the other is the Christ whose nude body is stretched on His mother's lap and balanced by the ample draping of the lower part of the Virgin's robe so that the two figures are inscribed in a single, compact block. Today, as then, the Virgin's extreme youth is unsettling: it is unusual in this type of portrayal because it is inconsistent with the age of the dead Christ. There is no definite information concerning the reasons for this choice, but we can recall that, according to Condivi (1553), Michelangelo argued that chaste women remain young longer than the unchaste, as if to suggest that Mary's purity could be visually translated into her enduring youth.

Michelangelo completed the *Pietà* in just one year, it was finished in 1499 the year that the patron died. The *Pietà* would become a constant theme in Michelangelo's sculpture. His statue attained such fame that it became a model for his contemporaries and for subsequent generations of artists. Raphael was among the first, drawing his inspiration from the *Pietà* for the *Baglioni Altarpiece* (Rome, Galleria Borghese). Later artists such as Caravaggio and David would look to the statue and specifically Christ's arm in the *Deposition* (1602-1604; Rome, Pinacoteca Vaticana) and the *Death of Marat* (1793; Brussels, Musées Royaux des Beaux Arts), respectively.

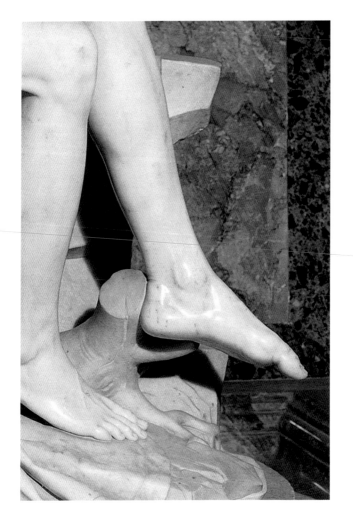

155

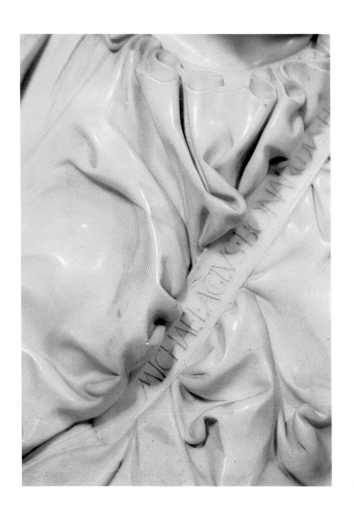

SCULPTURES FOR THE PICCOLOMINI ALTAR: SAINT PETER, SAINT PAUL, SAINT PIUS, SAINT GREGORY THE GREAT

In 1501 Michelangelo returned to Florence where, thanks to the advent of the gonfalonier Piero Soderini, an extraordinary, albeit brief, intellectual and artistic renaissance was occurring.

Probably the artist stopped in Siena on his way home to see the structure of the Piccolomini altar (Andrea Bregno, 1485) in the cathedral, and for which Buonarroti would have had to make some statues. The patron of the altar and sculptures was Francesco Todeschini Piccolimini, nephew of Pius II, who was elevated to Cardinal in 1460 and then became Pope Pius III in 1503. However, he died unexpectedly after only ten days as pope. Shortly before departing for Florence, Michelangelo had signed the contract in Rome in 1501 together with Todeschini and Jacopo Galli who acted as guarantor. The artist had three years to complete fifteen statues for the Siena altar for a payment of 500 ducats of which he received an advance of 100.

For Michelangelo this was a "minor" commission, certainly less gratifying than the one for the *David* that he received from the Operai del Duomo as soon as he arrived in Florence in August of the same year and that would be followed by many other prestigious contracts. It is significant that neither Condivi nor Vasari mention the Piccolomini sculptures in their biographies of the

FRAN·PICCOLOM·CAR·SENEN   PII·II·PONT·MAX·NEPOS·

artist. Michelangelo soon stopped work on the fifteen statues, he only completed four and delivered them in 1504: the apostles *Peter* and *Paul* and the two ecclesiastical saints *Pius* and *Gregory*. His failure to fulfill his obligations weighed on his conscience throughout his life to the point that at the age of eighty-six he still regretted his outstanding debt. It was paid by his nephew, Leonardo, after the artist's death.

The *Saint Paul* is certainly the finest of the four statues: he clutches his garments and is withdrawn into himself with a restlessness reminiscent of the *Saint Proculus* in Bologna (see pages 126-135) on the one hand, and of the prophets by Jacopo della Quercia on the baptismal font in the Siena cathedral on the other. The *Saint Peter* is much more tranquil, in both the serene face and the orderly folds of the draping he bears a greater resemblance to the *Four Crowned Saints* by Nanni di Banco (Orsanmichele, Florence).

On page 165,
Piccolomini Altar
Siena, Cathedral.

Saint Peter,
1501-1504,
marble, height 124 cm:
Siena, Cathedral, Piccolomini Altar.

Saint Paul,
1501-1504,
marble, height 127 cm;
Siena, Cathedral, Piccolomini Altar.

Saint Pius,
1501-1504,
marble, height 134 cm;
Siena, Cathedral, Piccolomini Altar.

Saint Gregory the Great,
1501-1504,
marble, height 132 cm;
Siena, Cathedral, Piccolomini Altar.

DAVID

In 1501 the twenty-six year old Michelangelo received a commission from the Florentine Republic. He was to carve a gigantic statue of David, the young shepherd who defeated the giant Goliath and went on to become king of Israel. Florence in those years – after the artistic and cultural stasis of Savonarola's rule that ended with his execution in 1498 – was experiencing a new phase of vitality and vigorously promoted initiatives, especially from 1502 on when Piero Soderini was elected gonfalonier for life.

To tell the truth, the colossal block of Carrara marble used for the *David* had been quarried years earlier and had already been the object of great interest on the part of the Florence's governors and artists who had often thought of using it for a sculpture of a magnitude never before seen in the city, to compete with ancient statuary. In 1464 the task was assigned to Agostino di Duccio but the contract was cancelled for unknown reasons. In 1475 the commission was given to Antonio Rossellino who roughed it without ever completing the statue. When Michelangelo accepted the assignment to carve a *David* the marble had been sitting in the storage areas of the Opera del Duomo, the institution in charge of the architectural and decorative works on the cathedral that had been completed with Brunelleschi's prodigious dome slightly more than fifty years before. The gigantic statue was to be placed on one of the buttresses of Santa Maria

David,
1501-1504,
marble, height 517 cm;
Florence, Galleria dell'Accademia.

del Fiore, hence the need for a huge statue that would be readily visible from the ground. Michelangelo agreed to complete the work in two years, for a payment of six gold florins per month. However, things dragged out, both because it was a difficult task to begin with and because the marble was streaked with veins (especially where the legs are) that increased the risk of breaking, and finally because working on something already started by others rather than a block of virgin stone made things even more difficult. Michelangelo, who preferred working alone without help, faced years of hard work, dealing with a difficult material, closed off from view by a screen improvised with what he found in a just as improvised workshop set up in the warehouses of the Opera near the cathedral. Month after month he worked night and day, often catching a few hours of sleep on the floor, without ever leaving his statue. Michelangelo finally completed his white "Giant" in 1504 (Condivi, 1553).

The first person to see the statue was the gonfalonier Pier Soderini, and Vasari records the episode in a famous anecdote (1568). While impressed by the sight, the Florentine notable said to Buonarroti "that is seemed to him that the nose of the figure was too thick." Michelangelo climbed up on the scaffolding, grabbed his chisel and a little marble dust from the planks, struck lightly with the tool and let the dust fall, leading Soderini, who could not actually see, to believe that he had, indeed modified the nose. Unknowing, but satisfied the gonfalonier said "You have given it life."

In fact, everyone believed that the grandiose statue of the Biblical hero, David, who won an impossible challenge against the immense and brutal Goliath, was the unexpected fruit of just as impossible a challenge – between the artist and the colossal block of marble. Such a monumental statue had not been seen since antiquity: the vista of the masterpiece seemed a "miracle" as "if the dead had been resurrected" (Vasari 1568). The *David* was so magnificent and grandiose that its original destination immediately seemed inadequate, so a debate began as to the most suitable place for this masterpiece. Soderini thought of placing it in Piazza della Signoria, the center of the city's political life. The statue would thus acquire a civil and political meaning, David who fought for the freedom of his people was the perfect incarnation of Republican virtue. But the exact position still had to be decided, so a committee was appointed, comprising some of the era's famous artists – Giuliano da Sangallo, Filippino Lip-

pi and Leonardo da Vinci. However, other questions came up: beneath the Loggia dell'Orcagna (later known as the Loggia dei Lanzi) or, as others proposed, in full view right in front of Palazzo della Signoria – which Michelangelo himself preferred and officially sanctioned on 25 January 1504. The work for moving the statue to the piazza began on 14 May and lasted for four days, hindered by protests and stone throwing. Then it was extremely difficult to place the statue where Donatello's *Judith* stood on the dais next to the entrance. It was finally completed on 8 June. While the pedestal was being built, Michelangelo was still busy with final touches on the statue which was unveiled on 8 September.

On 30 July 1873, following the Unification of Italy, the *David* made its second, difficult journey to the Galleria dell'Accademia, where it arrived on 8 August, when it was raised onto its existing pedestal in the Tribune that had been built specifically for that purpose. Thus the original was protected from atmospheric agents.

A copy was placed in front of Palazzo della Signoria, and a bronze reproduction was raised at Piazzale Michelangelo (1910). The new acquisition led to the construction of a Tribune in the museum, appropriate for Michelangelo's masterpiece. The plans by the architect Emilio De Fabris – who completed the Tribune between 1872 and 1882 – called for a Latin cross shaped room with a circular skylight above the *David*. In 1875, two years after the statue had been moved to the Accademia, the

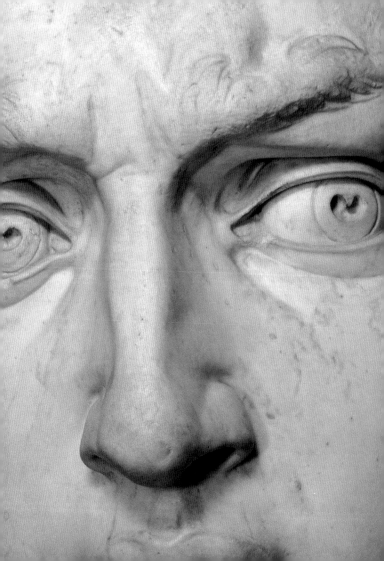

Tribune (though still unfinished) was selected as the ideal venue for the grand exhibition of reproductions of works by the artist for the four-hundredth anniversary celebrations of his birth.

Early in the XX century, however, the casts of Michelangelo's statues that framed the original *David* began to seem inappropriate. The decision was made to devote the museum to originals. In 1909 the *Slaves* which up to then had been in Buontalenti's grotto in the Boboli Gardens (see pages 318-335) and the *Saint Matthew* (see pages 214-219) from the courtyard of the Accademia di Belle Arti were brought to the Galleria; then in the late thirties, from the city from which the sculpture gets its name, the *Pietà di Palestrina* (see pages 102-103) also arrived in the museum, although today most historians no longer attribute this statue to Michelangelo.

The *David* was recently cleaned and restored (completed in 2004).

From an iconographic standpoint Michelangelo's *David* is clearly different from earlier Florentine renderings, the most famous of which are the *David* by Donatello and the *David* by Verrocchio (see pages 39 and 44). Donatello's hero has boots, helmet and sword; Verrocchio's also has a sword and boots and is wearing a light garment (in keeping with the Biblical description). Their bodies are fragile and youthfully immature, and Goliath's head is at their feet. Michelangelo's *David,* on the other hand, is nude, like a Greek god, he has only the sling on his left shoulder, his mission has not yet been fulfilled (Goliath's head is missing). Michelangelo portrayed him in the moments preceding the combat, visualizing the tension of the moment in the face, in the concentrated gaze, in the muscles ready to spring, in the tension of the hand hanging down along his leg. Michelangelo's seems to be a meditated choice, and from documents concerning the *David* we learn that he had originally been asked to adorn the hero with a crown of golden leaves and a gilded belt, that is a more traditional representation. Instead, the sculptor interpreted his *David* as an ideal man, clearly based on classical statuary even though it is impossible to indicate an exact model, thereby renewing the dictates of modern sculpture which, similarly to what was happening in other fields, was manifested through an aware and original return to the past. Michelangelo's *David* is not the hero of an event, he is the symbol of the civilization in which he was conceived, the sublime epitome of virtue.

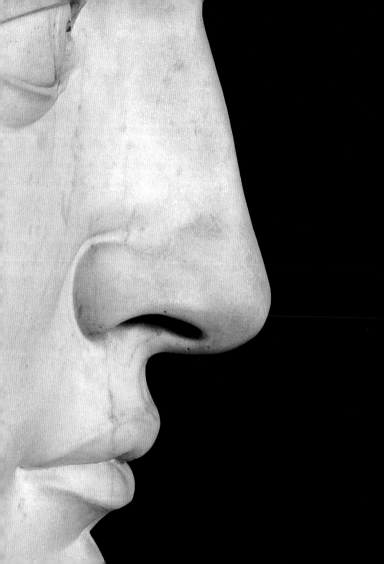

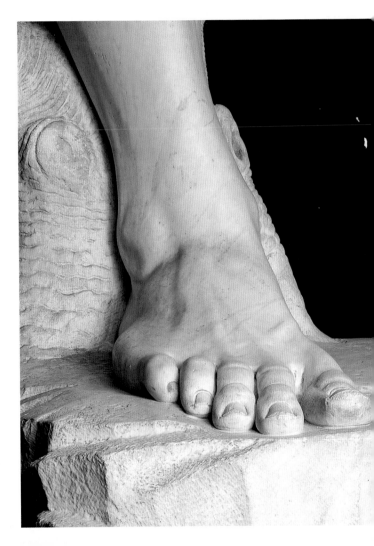

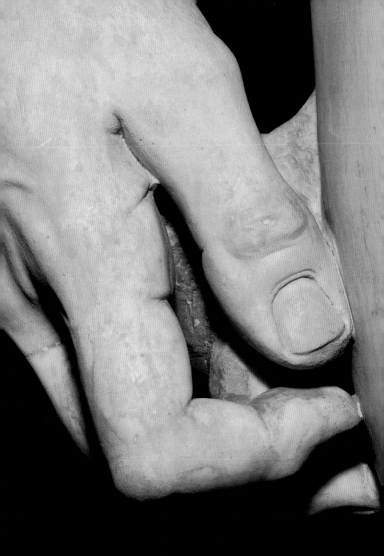

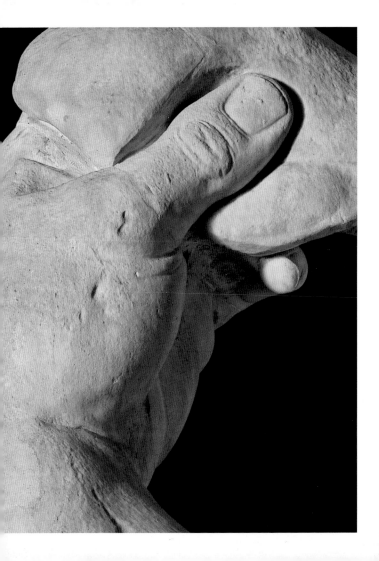

BRUGES MADONNA

This *Virgin and Child* had been commissioned by two Flemish merchants, Jean and Alexander Mouscron, for the family's burial chapel in the cathedral of Notre Dame in Bruges. There was a flourishing trade in textiles at the time between Flanders and Florence, and Michelangelo's commission was not the only case of cultural exchange. The Mouscrons had been clients of the Balducci-Galli bank in Rome since 1501 and it is likely that once again Jacopo Galli acted as intermediary for this commission.

Carved in Florence and paid for between 1503 and 1505 the sculpture had been seen by very few people. In a letter to his father in January 1506 Michelangelo urged him to take it to his home and not show it to anyone. This could, at least partly, explain the fact that both Vasari and Condivi speak of it such vague terms as to lead us to believe that they had very little information. In any event, Raphael did have an opportunity to see it before it was sent to Flanders – just in time to draw his inspiration for some of the solutions he used in the *Madonna of the Goldfinch* painted in 1507 (Florence, Uffizi). In a letter written in August 1506 Giovanni Balducci informed Michelangelo of the possibility of shipping the statue from the port of Leghorn to Bruges. Once in Bruges it was picked up by the heirs of the patrons who had died in the meantime and was placed in Notre Dame where Albrecht Dürer, the leading artist of the German Renaissance, saw it in 1521.

Virgin and Child
(*Bruges Madonna*),
c. 1503-1505,
marble, height 94 cm;
Bruges, Notre Dame (Onze-Lieve-Vrouwekerk).

The Virgin is seated on a rock, holding the Child between her knees as He tries to scamper off her lap and go down the step covered by her mantle. Her face recalls other female images by Botticelli and Benedetto da Maiano. The gazes of both Mary and Jesus are concentrated and focused on the distance, alluding to an awareness of the coming Passion and Redemption as written in the closed book of Scriptures in the Virgin's hand. Mary's mantle covering one shoulder of the Infant prefigures the shroud. The gestures with which the Child hold's his Mother's knee and the way Mary tightly holds onto Him while he is stepping down are intense expressions of her love and His need for protection.

TADDEI TONDO

The two marble tondos Michelangelo carved for Bartolomeo Pitti and Taddeo Taddei are chronologically close even though their respective datings are highly disputed. According to Vasari (1568), the *Taddei Tondo* was done before the *Pitti*.

In both tondos Michelangelo found himself dealing with a theme and a format – circular – that were quite usual in XV and early XVI century Florentine painting. He certainly was familiar with Luca Signorelli's *Virgin and Child* and the *Madonna of the Magnificat* by Botticelli that were the latest "advances" in the field. Marble relief tondos, however, were quite rare, some had been done by Benedetto da Maiano, probably one of Michelangelo's teachers. Furthermore, representations of the Virgin and Child and the Young Saint John, holding a goldfinch, symbol of the human soul, were quite popular in Florence since he is the city's patron saint. However, the sculptural innovation was the full-figure rendition in motion. In the *Taddei Tondo* the fleeting pose of the young Jesus expresses the Child's fear as the little Saint John presents him the animal (we cannot determine whether it really a goldfinch), prefiguring the Passion. The artist's formal solutions are the fruit of a personal rendering of Leonardo da Vinci's studies of the same theme – he too was in Florence from 1501 on. The *tondos* are unfinished and were not prepared for framing. Aside from any factors that may have prompted the

Virgin and Child with the Young Saint John
(*Taddei Tondo*),
c. 1504-1506,
Carrara marble, diameter c. 109 cm;
London, Royal Academy of Fine Arts.

artist to leave many works uncompleted, the two *tondos* prove that the Michelangelesque "un-finished" treatment has great expressive power indeed. In the *Taddei Tondo* we can see how the meticulous finishing of the Virgin and Child contrasts with the roughness of the background as if to create an atmosphere of pictorial indetermination also evoking an indistinct darkness from which the figures emerge.

Raphael saw the tondo in the Taddeo Taddei's home, and before departing for Rome in 1508 he copied it and drew inspiration for sketches and paintings (*Bridgewater Madonna*, 1506-1508, Edinburgh, National Gallery of Scotland).

PITTI TONDO

The *Taddei* and *Pitti* tondos were completed in a relatively short period, between 1503 and 1504. Bartolomeo Pitti was the patron who commissioned the sculpture that is now in the Bargello. He was belonged to one of the city's oldest noble families, was an Operaio di Santa Maria del Fiore and had dealings with the artist for the statues of the apostles for the cathedral (see page 56). Michelangelo never completed the tondo, most probably because he had to leave for Rome in 1503 to work on the Monument to Julius II.

Virgin and Child with the Young Saint John
(*Pitti Tondo*),
c. 1503-1505,
marble, 85.5 x 82 cm;
Florence, Museo Nazionale del Bargello.

As we have already mentioned regarding the *Taddei Tondo* (see pages 204-207) Michelangelo dealt with the traditional tondo in completely original terms, both as regards the use of sculpture – an unusual technique for the shape – and his full-figure portrayals.

Both compositions present the Virgin Mary as a "Madonna of Humility" seated on the ground, in the *Pitti Tondo* she is crouching on a low plinth. She stands out against the background with more monumentality than the Virgin in the *Taddei Tondo,* to the point that her head reaches above the barely roughed frame. Notwithstanding the apparent naturalness with which she sits on her cubic seat, she barely fits into the circular field. The cherub on the headband is an *unicum* among the Marian headdresses of the period, while the position of the Baby Jesus has been compared to that of an ancient funerary spirit.

In this case the unfinished background served to conceal one of Michelangelo's *pentimenti:* originally he had planned on showing a three-quarter view of the Child's face, but then decided to turn it so that it is practically in profile. The head of the young Saint John, partly hidden by the Virgin's shoulder is carved in very low- relief. With his wind-tousled hair he recalls the *putti* in the *cantorias* of the Florence cathedral made seventy years earlier by Donatello and Luca della Robbia.

SAINT MATTHEW

In 1503 Michelangelo undertook to carve a series of twelve apostles for the Opera del Duomo, the larger than life-size statues were to be placed in niches inside the cathedral. However, the contract was terminated a few years later because of the artist's other commitments and the *Saint Matthew* is the only statue he made. And even though it is unfinished, nothing detracts from its expressive power and its perfection.

The accentuated contraposition of the left knee and right shoulder, the twisting of the head seem natural movements for the apostle trying to emerge from the rough block of marble that holds him almost a prisoner. Thanks to this interpretation, that reflects the concept of sculpture that Michelangelo often reiterated in his writings, the statue actually seems complete. Furthermore, it offers a precise idea of how he actually worked. Vasari and Condivi report that he usually prepared a drawing for one side of the marble block and then began working only on that side so that the figure would gradually come to the surface, as if coming out of a tub of water.

Saint Matthew,
c. 1503-1506,
marble, height 216 cm;
Florence, Galleria dell'Accademia.

In the tense and contrasting pose of Saint Matthew and his grieving expression there is a reference to the *Laocoon* (Musei Vaticani), an impressive, Hellenistic marble group depicting the priest of Troy and his sons trying to defend themselves against the serpents sent by Neptune (see pages 69 and 72). The statue, celebrated by Pliny was found in Rome during excavations in a vineyard near Santa Maria Maggiore in 1506, just when Michelangelo was in the city. Giuliano da Sangallo who was there at the time of the find urgently summoned Michelangelo so that he could admire the piece, an extraordinary and powerful portrayal of *pathos*.

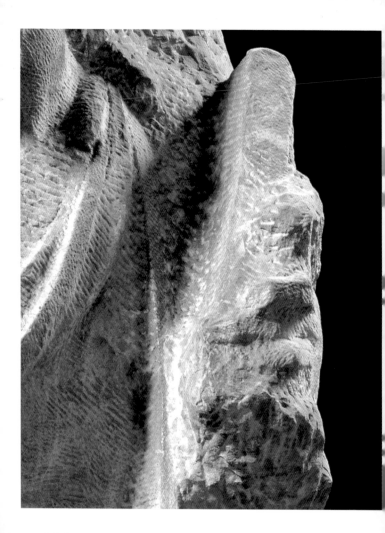

Sculptures for the Monument to Julius II: the Dying Slave and the Rebellious Slave

Michelangelo carved the two *Slaves* that are now in the Louvre between 1513 and 1516 for the second version of the Monument to Julius II, as agreed with the pope's heirs in 1513. Since they were not used, in 1546 he gave them to his friend, Roberto Strozzi who took them to France, where, in 1794, they were purchased by the Louvre. In the XIX century the statues were named the *Dying Slave* and the *Rebellious Slave,* with romantic interpretations.

The first contract for the huge project dated from 1505, when Pope Julius II himself personally summoned Michelangelo to design and build his funeral monument, that was to stand in the choir of the new Saint Peter's Basilica in the Vatican. The artist's ambitious project, that had been approved by the pope, called for a tomb like an ancient mausoleum, free-standing on all four sides with forty statues and countless bronze reliefs. It was designed with three registers, decreasing in size upwards: at the bottom there were to be pairs of statues depicting *Victories,* or Good conquering *Moses, Saint Paul,* the *Active Life* and the *Contemplative Life,* and finally the structure was to be crowned by the sarcophagus containing the pope's mortal remains flanked by two statues which, according to Vasari (1568) represented the Earth Grieving

Dying Slave,
c. 1513,
marble, height 229 cm;
Paris, Louvre.

over the pontiff's death, and Heaven Rejoicing because his soul had arrived.

This project was never completed because the pope changed his mind – and for a short time – had broken off his relationship with the artist who was then busy painting the frescoes in the Sistine chapel (see pages 73-74). In 1513, after the pope's death, another contract was drawn up with his heirs. This marked the beginning of the gradual reduction of the scale of the monument – both its size and the number of statues; the project continued for years and only ended in 1545 with the Monument in San Pietro in Vincoli (see pages 72-73).

The new contract, signed on 6 May 1513, after the approval of the models the artist had submitted, called for placing the four-sided, two-tiered structure against a wall. The themes of the statues were more or less than same, and the narrative bas-reliefs were reduced to three. In addition to the two *Slaves* in 1513 the plans included the *Moses* which is in the completed, final version of the monument in San Pietro in Vincoli.

The theme of the *Slaves* fascinated Michelangelo and allowed him to express fundamental aspects of his poetics and at the same time to display his formal, inventive skills. The complex, twisted, pained motion of the grandiose figures prompted fruitful comparisons with ancient masterpieces such as the Belvedere *Torso* and the *Laocoon* discovered in Rome in 1506.

The *Dying Slave* is one of Michelangelo's greatest and most complete tributes to male beauty. The pose is languid and sensual; the body truly creates the impression of sliding down along the wall on which it was supposed to be placed. The raised arm recalls the iconography of the martyrdom of Saint Sebastian. The bands on the chest and wrists are often interpreted as chains, but they do not impede movement in any way. Behind the legs there is a monkey with a barely roughed mirror that would seem to confirm Condivi's interpretation (1553): it symbolizes the Arts (monkeys or apers of nature) that literally tied to death of Julius II.

The languid sensuality of the first *Slave* is countered by the energetic strength of the *Rebellious Slave* with arms tied behind his back. The powerful youth is leaning forward and twisting, with the left shoulder and the right knee in counterpoint. This statue probably was to have been at a corner of the monument, and this could explain the fact that the right shoulder is undefined and flat.

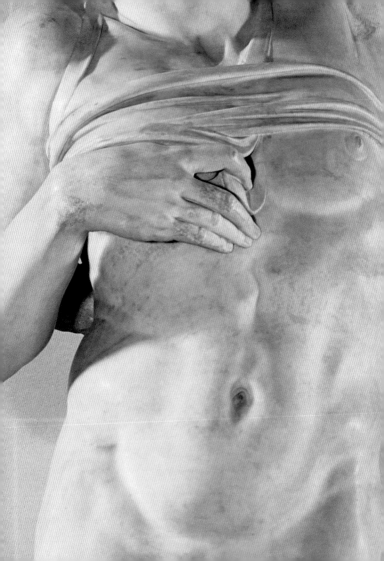

Rebellious Slave,
c. 1513,
marble, height 215 cm;
Paris, Louvre.

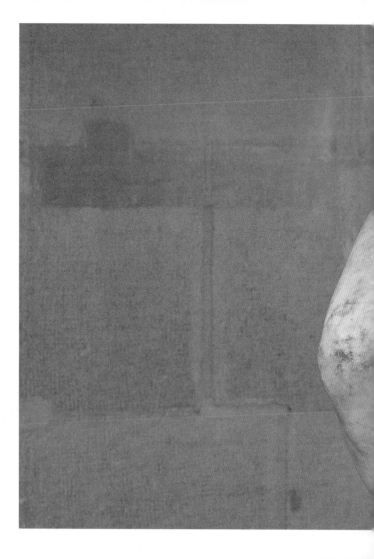

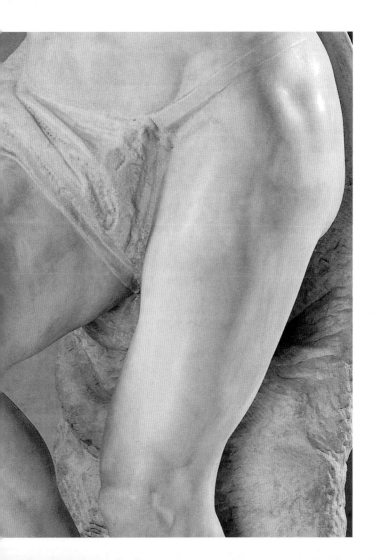

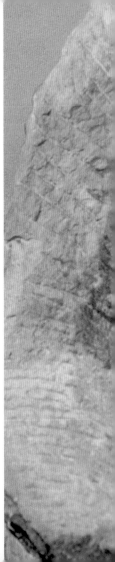

Moses

Michelangelo carved the *Moses* by the end of 1516 working in his house at Macel de' Corvi in Rome. The statue was destined for the Monument to Julius II, in Saint Peter's Basilica according to the plans in the second contract signed with the pope's heirs in 1513. He had already completed the *Slaves* that are now in the Louvre (see entry for more details on the general plans and design, pages 220-231). As opposed to the two sculptures in Paris, Michelangelo actually did use the *Moses* in the final version of the monument that was erected in San Pietro in Vincoli between 1542 and 1545, and made some changes to the sculpture.

Moses,
1513-1516,
marble, height 235 cm; Rome,
San Pietro in Vincoli, Monument to Julius II.

The great *Moses* is one of the most famous masterpieces of Renaissance art, and was quickly admired for its power, its *terribilità,* by contemporaries to the extent that it was considered "divine." The character of the *Moses* is rendered in such an impressive way and has such universal value that, according to Vasari (1568) hoards of Roman Jews came to admire it even though it was in a Catholic church. Within the *corpus* of Michelangelo's works, the *Moses* is almost a sculptural translation of one of the *Prophets* he frescoed on the ceiling of the Sistine Chapel. The statue was designed to be viewed from below, since it was to be on the second tier of the structure he designed in 1513. For this reason Michelangelo elongated the torso and tilted it forward to make the head more readily visible. The vigorous strength of the lower limbs is highlighted by the rich folds of the robes and the position of the legs ready to raise the figure to a standing position.

The fingers are between the locks of the long, flowing beard, a passage of technical and expressive virtuosity. The right arm holds the tables of the Law against his side. The head is turned to the left in a sudden and clean movement guided by the intense and focused gaze. Following an ancient iconography Michelangelo portrayed Moses with horns due to an error in the Latin translation of the Bible that was handed down for generations. Indeed, the appellative *cornutus* translates the Hebrew word that means radiant referring to Moses, who after he had received the Tables of the Law came down from Mt. Sinai with two rays of light beaming from his head.

Among earlier statues that may have inspired Michelangelo, there is certainly the *Saint John the Evangelist* that Donatello made in 1414 for the façade of Santa Maria del Fiore in Florence. With respect to the XV century statue, the *Moses* seems animated by a vital spark, by a bursting energy that makes it a much more live and unsettling presence.

THE RISEN CHRIST

In 1514 a group of Roman noblemen, including Metello Vari, commissioned Michelangelo to make a life-size statue of *Christ* standing with the cross, at the moment of the Resurrection. The sculpture was meant for the church of Santa Maria sopra Minerva. A first version of the statue was abandoned in 1516, when it was already near completion, because a vein in the marble became evident. This statue was recently identified as the sculpture in the sacristy of San Vicenzo Martire at Bassano Romano in the province of Viterbo (see pages 80-82).

Three years later, because of the patron's insistence Michelangelo, who was then in Florence working on the Fabbrica di San Lorenzo – began a new block of marble and nearly completed the *Risen Christ*. He sent the statue to Rome so that it could finished by a trusted assistant, Pietro Urbano. But, in 1521, the painter Sebastiano del Piombo wrote an alarmed letter to Michelangelo informing him that the assistant had been so clumsy as to irreparably damage the marble, and especially the fingers. The task was transferred to Federico Frizzi who also positioned the statue on 27 December of that same year. However, Michelangelo was never completely satisfied with the results and offered to make a new version, but Metello Vari refused.

The Risen Christ,
1519-1521,
marble, height 205 cm;
Rome, Santa Maria sopra Minerva.

In addition to the huge cross, the Redeemer holds other symbols of the Passion such as the vinegar-soaked sponge and the reed. The *Christ* that was probably covered with a draping from the beginning still presents a gilded metal cloth. And yet, in spite of this, the artist had defined the full nudity of the figure and conferred on it an ideal appearance of Apollonian beauty, totally free of religious mysticism.

The statue, that was supposed to stand in a niche, can be viewed from several points over 180°. The twisted position of the pelvis creates the opposing motion of the limbs, head and torso around the static axis of the vertical upright of the cross.

The Sculptures in the New Sacristy, San Lorenzo

In 1520 when the plans for the façade of San Lorenzo were abandoned, Pope Leo X and Cardinal Giulio de' Medici commissioned Michelangelo to build a chapel, the New Sacristy, adjacent to the right transept of the Basilica of San Lorenzo. It was called "New" to distinguish it from the Sacristy built by Brunelleschi in the left transept, one hundred years earlier. In San Lorenzo which is near the Medici Palace (today Palazzo Medici Riccardi) were the tombs of Cosimo the Elder and other members of the family. The New Sacristy was conceived to house the monumental tombs of the dynasty's younger members who had died early deaths: Giuliano Duke of Nemours (d. 1516) and Lorenzo Duke of Urbino (d. 1519), brother and nephew, respectively of Leo X.

Tomb of Giuliano Duke of Nemours,
c. 1526-1532,
Florence, Museo delle Cappelle Medicee,
San Lorenzo, New Sacristy.

Initially the idea was to build a single monument for four individuals which, in addition to the two dukes, would hold the remains of Lorenzo (d. 1492) and Giuliano de' Medici (d. 1478), known as "Magnificent." This project was soon abandoned in favor of the idea of building the monuments to the two dukes against the side walls and building a double monument for the two "Magnificent" men on the wall facing the altar.

Work on the Medici chapel was interrupted in 1527 when the Imperial army descended on Italy to sack Rome. Pope Clement VII fled to Orvieto and the Florentines once again revolted against the Medici government and established a second republic. Although Michelangelo had actively participated in the works on the fortifications to protect the city against a siege, after the Medici

Tomb of Giuliano Duke of Nemours
and the allegories of *Night* and *Day*,
c. 1526-1532,
Florence, Museo delle Cappelle Medicee,
San Lorenzo, New Sacristy.

returned in 1530 he was pardoned and was asked to resume work on the Medici Tombs. The New Sacristy was unfinished when Michelangelo definitively left Florence in 1534. Giorgio Vasari and Bartolomeo Ammannati completed the arrangement of the statues by order of Cosimo I de' Medici (1554-1555), who never managed to get the artist to give him precise instructions for his unfinished works, nor did he succeed in bringing him back to Florence.

Giuliano Duke of Nemours,
c. 1526-1532,
marble, height 173 cm;
Florence, Museo delle Cappelle Medicee,
San Lorenzo, New Sacristy.

The chapel is distinguished from earlier noble chapels by the close bond between the statuary and the architecture that merge into a unity of visual arts never seen before that date (regarding the architecture see also the entry on pages 396-399). Indeed, even though the architectural cladding and the statuary remained incomplete and the gilded and white stucco grotesques by Giovanni da Udine that decorated the coffers on the dome have been lost, the New Sacristy is still the most complete and emblematic of Michelangelo's achievements where even today architecture, sculpture and decorations comprise a whole that dialectically evokes the artist's poetics. Subsequent generations of artist, at least to the end of the century, were inspired by studies of the whole and each detail.

The tombs of the dukes are set against the lateral walls. Each of the two sarcophagi is decorated with two allegories of the *Times of Day* on the lid and the image of the deceased in the niche above. Giuliano Duke of Nemours is watched over by *Night* and *Day*, while *Dusk* and *Dawn* are with Lorenzo the Duke of Urbino: these are four personifications that had never been portrayed before – in ancient or contemporary art. The structure of the tombs also presents important innovations with respect to styles used up to then. None of the earlier Medici Tombs in San Lorenzo had portraits of the deceased, even though portraits were used between the XIV and XV centuries. Generally the statues of the deceased were reclining or lying down with eyes closed. In the New Sacristy the two Captains are seated in niches, dressed in ancient-style armor and clearly inspired (especially Giuliano) by Imperial Roman iconography. In most cases Renaissance sarcophagi

Tomb of Giuliano Duke of Nemours,
detail, *Night*,
c. 1526-1531,
Carrara marble, length 194 cm;
Florence, Museo delle Cappelle Medicee,
San Lorenzo, New Sacristy.

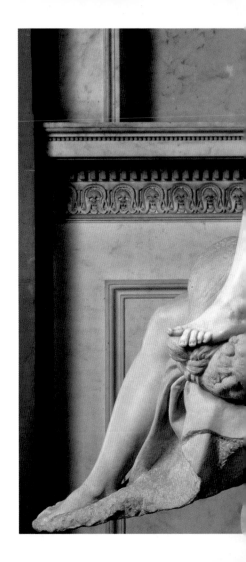

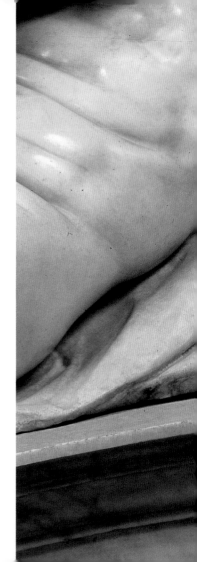

had flat lids, to hold a statue of the dead: here the innovation was the rounded shape decorated with scrolls and reclining allegorical figures in a seemingly unstable balance. Even more unusual is the fact there is no inscription or epitaph on the tombs, not even the Medici coat of arms. If on the one hand this is proof of the great freedom the artist had in creating the tombs, on the other it makes it difficult to identify the figures. In this regard, on a sheet with preparatory drawings for the two tombs (London, British Museum, inv. n. 1859-6-25-543) Michelangelo had written that Fame cannot celebrate the exploits of the two captains because they are dead and their work interrupted ("*La fama tiene gli epitaffi a giacere; non va né innanzi né indientro, perché son morti, e el loro operare è*

fermo"). We do know that the artist was criticized because his sculptures do not resemble the subjects, but he replied that it was unimportant since within a few years no one would remember what they looked like

Giuliano Duke of Nemours (1526-1532 c.) is portrayed with a baton in his right hand because he led a pontifical army, and a coin in his left. He seems ready to spring as he faces the back of the chapel. This is revealed by the elongated neck and focused gaze. He is contracted, ready to stand up and act. The pose recalls the solution Michelangelo had already used in the *Moses* (see pages 232-243). On the sarcophagus are *Day* and *Night* (c. 1526-1531) with bodies twisted in opposite directions to each other. In a note written on a sheet together with studies for the sculpture (Florence, Casa Buonarroti, inv. 10A), Michelangelo explains the meaning of these allegories: "The

Tomb of Giuliano Duke of Nemours,
detail, *Day*,
c. 1526-1531,
Carrara marble, length 285 cm;
Florence, Museo delle Cappelle Medicee,
San Lorenzo, New Sacristy.

Day and Night speak and say: We have with our swift flight led the Duke Giuliano to his death, and it is appropriate that he avenge himself. And this is the revenge: that we having killed him, he in death has taken the light and closed our eyes that no longer shine on earth. What would he have done to us while he was alive?"

Day has a powerful body and an indistinct face with a still rugged surface, as if caused by blinding light from which he seems to defend himself with his shoulder and arm. *Night* with a flaccid stomach rests her foot on a bunch of poppies, wears a crown with a crescent moon and a star; a hollow-eyed mask of dreams and an owl are next to her. *Night* in its complex, left-right pose was inspired by the iconography of the *Leda and the Swan* that Michelangelo may have seen on a precious ancient gem mentioned in a 1492 inventory of Lorenzo the Magnificent's property and now conserved the Museo Archeologico in Naples. Michelangelo also returned to

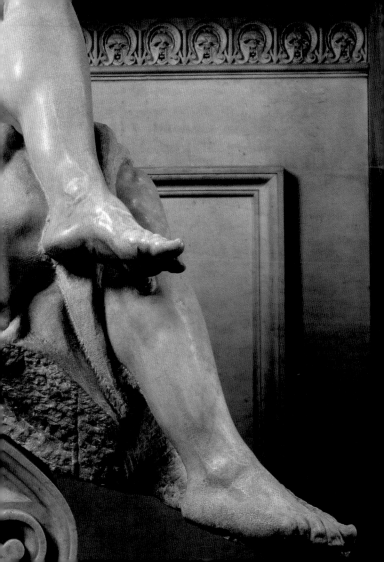

the theme in a cartoon (lost) for Alfonso d'Este, and there are some engravings made from it. After a recent restoration the polished surface of the marble seems much lighter than that of the other three, revealing a cold, shining candor that recalls the effects of moonbeams. Giovanni Battista Strozzi, leader of the republican faction opposing the Medici, described *Night* in the New Sacristy in a famous quatrain quoted by Giorgio Vasari (1550, 1568): "*La Notte che tu vedi in sì dolci atti / dormire, fu da un Angelo scolpita / in questo sasso; e perché dorme, ha vita / déstala, se nol credi e parleratti*". Michelangelo rendered his response in melancholy lines: "*Caro m'è il sonno, e più l'esser di sasso / mentre che il danno e la vergogna dura: / non veder, non sentir, m'è gran ventura, / però non mi destar, deh parla basso*". These are lines that recall the dramatic moments following the 1529-1530 siege of Florence and the defeat of the last republic.

Tomb of Lorenzo Duke of Urbino,
and the allegories of *Dawn* and *Dusk*,
c. 1525-1531;
Florence, Museo delle Cappelle Medicee,
San Lorenzo, New Sacristy.

The statue of *Lorenzo de' Medici* begun around 1525 was defined by Vasari as "pensive" hence the current appellative "Thoughtful" from his meditative pose that contrasts with *Giuliano*, who is bold and ready for action. The objects are of uncertain meaning: the kerchief in hand and the box with the bat's head beneath the elbow, which if it contained money could be an allusion to his generosity. His face, half-concealed by the imaginative, lion-shaped helmet is intent on the back wall and the tombs of his ancestors.

Lorenzo Duke of Urbino,
c. 1525-1526,
Carrara marble, length 178 cm;
Florence, Museo delle Cappelle Medicee,
San Lorenzo, New Sacristy.

In the statue of *Dawn* (1525-1526 c.) in 1550 Vasari had already noted "In her attitude may be seen her effort, as she rises, heavy with sleep, and raises herself from her downy bed; and it seems that in awakening she has found the eyes of that great Duke closed in death..." Indeed, the woman seems to make an effort to get up, and her grieved and bitter expression, is typical of one who meets all the afflictions of life upon rising.

Dawn and *Night* were praised by contemporary critics because the artist had "given the female bodies male muscles" according to Pietro Aretino. Because of the powerful musculature and proportions and complex articulation of the shapes these sculptures clearly represent Michelangelo's ideal of female beauty as formulated in his works and it corresponds to the esthetic principles set forth in contemporary treatises.

Dawn's counterpart on the other tomb is *Dusk* that gradually seems to let its limbs slide downwards. The statues on the tombs of the Medici captains correspond to a

Tomb of Lorenzo Duke of Urbino,
detail, *Dawn,*
c. 1525-1526,
Carrara marble, length 206 cm;
Florence, Museo delle Cappelle Medicee,
San Lorenzo, New Sacristy.

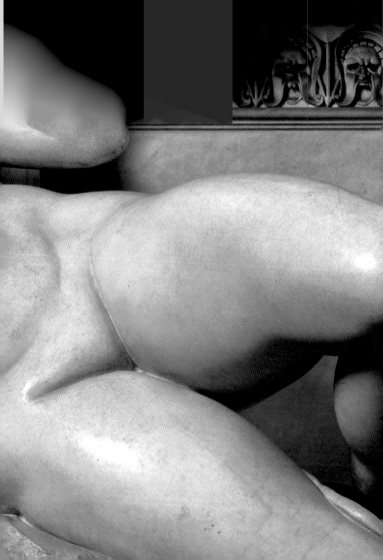

series of opposing and crossed references. In fact, the *Times of Day* comply with the ideal diagonal lines, in the man-woman pair on each tomb and from tomb to tomb. Furthermore, they present contrasting motion: *Day* and *Night* rotate, while *Dawn* and *Dusk* move vertically – up and down

Giuliano Duke of Nemours and *Lorenzo Duke of Urbino* are looking towards the wall opposite the altar, in the direction of the *Madonna and Child,* the spiritual and emotion fulcrum of the entire complex, which according to Michelangelo's designs was to be set in a niche above the tombs of the two men known as "Magnificent." In

their place today there is a single chest that serves as the pedestal for the statue. Carved in 1521 and left in little more than a roughed state, the *Madonna and Child* presents a twisting dynamic of two bodies: the Mother is elongated and articulated along broken diagonals, with legs crossed she seems to be in a precarious equilibrium; the Child is turned towards her, seeking her breast, concealing His face and creating a sense of spiral motion. The Virgin is flanked by *Saints Cosmas and Damian,* protectors of the Medici house, in adoration: the two sculptures were made to the master's models by Giovanni Angelo Montorsoli (c. 1537) and Raffaello da Montelupo (1531) respectively.

As we can see from Michelangelo's studies, the dukes' tombs were to have been accompanied by reclining statues of *Rivers* (the rivers of the underworld) placed on

Tomb of Lorenzo Duke of Urbino,
detail, *Dusk,*
c. 1526-1531
Carrara marble, length 195 cm;
Florence, Museo delle Cappelle Medicee,
San Lorenzo, New Sacristy.

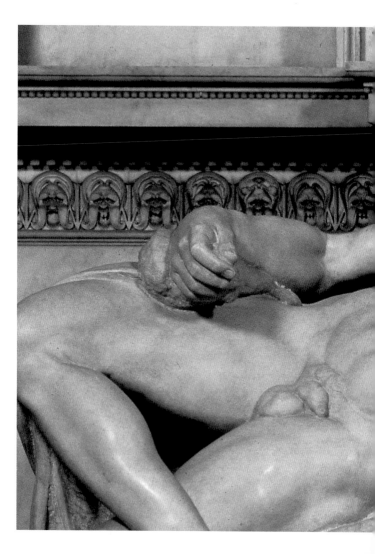

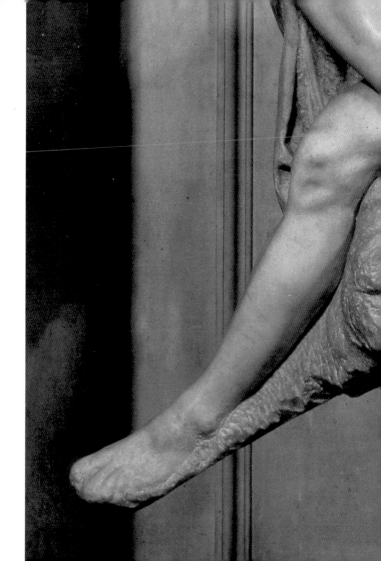

the sides of the bottom step at the foot of the tombs. These sculptures were never made, even if a partial, full-scale clay model still remains in Casa Buonarroti (see pages 304-307) The niches on either side of the deceased were to have hosted other, probably allegorical, statues. Perhaps the personification of *Earth Weeping* for his death and *Heaven Rejoicing* for his arrival were to have been next to Giuliano, while the identity of the statues flanking Lorenzo is still a mystery. Each upper level was to have held an antique style trophy and other statues of grief, that probably included the *Crouching Youth* now in the Hermitage in St. Petersburg (see pages 308-311).

Virgin and Child (Medici Madonna),
c. 1526-1534,
Carrara marble, height 226 cm;
Florence, Museo delle Cappelle Medicee,
San Lorenzo, New Sacristy.

Tomb of Giuliano
Duke of Nemours
and *Virgin and Child*
between *Saints Cosmas*
and *Damian*, Florence,
Museo delle Cappelle
Medicee, San Lorenzo,
New Sacristy.

LORENZO IL MAGNIFICO E GIULIANO DEI MEDICI

Considering the unfinished nature of the New Sacristy, it is very difficult to provide a convincing symbolic interpretation of the chapel. On the one hand it is so enigmatic and fascinating that it has given rise to the most varied hypotheses, including the highly accredited one in Neoplatonic key. According to this theory the architectural structure with its statues would recall the journey of dead souls: from the underworld represented by the *Rivers* that were to have stood on the daises beneath the sarcophagi, to earthly existence symbolized by the *Times of Day*, to the timeless dimension of contemplation of the divine in which the Dukes and Captains and their protector saints turn their adoring eyes to the *Madonna and Child*. The contrast between the personalities of Giuliano and Lorenzo is considered the antithesis between active and meditative – the Jovian and the Saturnian – one of the pillars of Neoplatonic doctrine. The heavenly sphere would have been symbolized by the attic and the vault of the chapel.

From Michelangelo's notes on the sheets with studies for the Sacristy and contemporary biographies we see a substantial basis for the iconography in the overall theme of "Time that consumes all", that nibbles and devours, like the mouse that Michelangelo wanted to include among the sculptures in the New Sacristy as an allegory, but was prevented from doing so (Condivi 1553).

RIVER GOD

The *River God*, in Casa Buonarroti, is the only full-scale model Michelangelo made that has come down to us. It is the final plan for one of the four river gods that he was to have placed at the feet and on the sides of the tombs of *Lorenzo Duke of Urbino* and *Giuliano Duke of Nemours* in the New Sacristy (see pages 250-303) The preparatory drawings for the Medici tombs in the New Sacristy show that the sculpture based on this model was to have been situated on the dais of the monument to Lorenzo on the left. According to ancient iconography the personifications of the Rivers were reclining male nudes surrounded by symbols of fertility such as putti holding jars for pouring water. Michelangelo may have been aware of important iconographic precedents such as the *Marforio* or *Tiber* known since the Middle Ages (Rome, Musei Capitolini) and the *Belvedere Nile* found in 1513 (Musei Vaticani).

The artist did not usually make full-scale models, but he had to make an exception for the New Sacristy as it had been requested by Pope Clement VII who, however, did allow Michelangelo to delegate part of the work to assistants and pupils. The models of the *Rivers* for the New Sacristy were placed in the positions destined for the final sculptures, probably to see how the whole would look. Two of those models, including this one in Casa Buonarroti were still in place in the middle of the XVI century.

River God,
c. 1524-1527,
unfired clay, river sand, animal skins,
plant fibers, wood, wire and metal mesh,
height 65 x 140 x 70 cm;
Florence, Casa Buonarroti.

CROUCHING YOUTH

This statue, considered one of the Hermitage museum's great masterpieces, portrays a crouching boy with a curved back, looking down with his face hidden, and hands on the ground. Today, following confirmations and checks published in a recent exhibit (2000) it is generally accepted as Michelangelo's autography. The statue, which is roughed and barely modeled, seems to be inspired by ancient sculptures such as the *Spinario* and the *Arrotino* that were already part of the Medici collections and the *Belvedere Torso* that Michelangelo had seen at the pontifical court.

Crouching Youth,
c. 1530-1534,
marble, height 54 cm;
Saint Petersburg, Hermitage.

Conceived around 1521, the statue of the youth was to have been placed – along with other similar pieces – in the lateral niches of the attic above the tombs of the dukes and captains in the New Sacristy as we can see from a plan of the tomb of Giuliano Duke of Nemours in the British Museum in London (inv. 1859.5-14-823). Figures of crouching men on either side of the trophy were to represent grief over the Medici deaths – or according to another interpretation – those defeated by the military prowess of the deceased. According to one recent hypothesis (Androsov 2000), Michelangelo may have carved the statue between 1530 and 1534 when he had already decided not to include it in the Medici Chapel – perhaps for a new, and still unknown, destination (if there was one). In particular if he had carved the *Youth* during the months of forced isolation following the definitive defeat of the Republic and the return of the Medicis (1530), it is easy to imagine that the artist projected the anguish of those days dramatic days of defeat and uncertainty into the figure of the grieving youth.

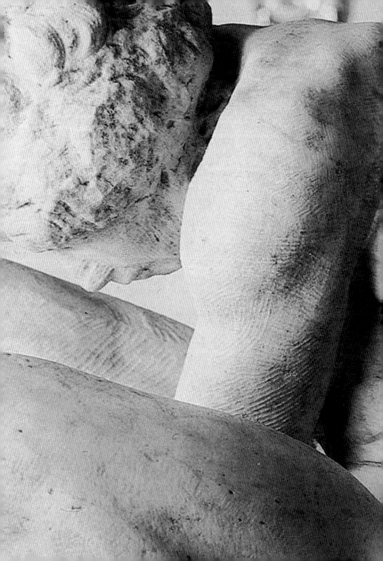

DAVID-APOLLO

Vasari (1550 and 1568) tells us that after returning to Florence from Ferrara and Venice in November 1529 "... [for] Baccio Valori [he] began a figure of three braccia in marble, which was an Apollo drawing an arrow from his quiver." After August 1530, when the Florentine Republic fell, Pope Clement VII appointed Baccio Valori, who was Apostolic administrator of the papal troops, governor of Florence, that had definitely returned to the Medici rule. With that statue Michelangelo tried to regain the favor of the Medicis even though he had openly fought on behalf of the Republic. In a letter datable 1531-1532, the patron asked the artist to complete the statue he had been awaiting for some time. Work was interrupted and we do not know if it ever reached Baccio Valori's palazzo, he was decapitated in 1537, but it is certain that in 1533 it was recorded in the collection of Cosimo I de' Medici and described as a "David."

David-Apollo,
c. 1530-1531,
marble, height 146 cm;
Florence, Museo Nazionale del Bargello.

The doubtful identify is due to the incomplete nature of the statue and the barely roughed features. It has even been hypothesized that artist began with a *David* and then transformed it into an *Apollo*. Apart from the subject, the position of the figure, gently turning on itself in a serpentine movement, with the torso tilted slightly backward to conclude in the idealized face, looking back, was an important inspiration for XVI century art.

THE SLAVES

Michelangelo carved the four *Slaves* while he was in Florence working on San Lorenzo, perhaps a few years before he returned to Rome when he had resumed work on the New Sacristy under orders from Clement VII. He worked on the immense statues to include them in a new and reduced version of the Della Rovere tomb, as set forth in the contract with the family signed in 1516, that is, with twenty-two statues instead of forty. He then abandoned the sculptures in 1532 following the new contract that required only six statues. Michelangelo stated that he had four of the six requested pieces in his Rome studio (the *Moses,* the *Slaves* now in the Louvre and perhaps the *Julius II*). Back in his Florentine workshop on Via Mozza he had to stop working on the four *Slaves* to concentrate on the two-figure group of *Victory* (see pages 342-349). In 1534 when he left for Rome the *Slaves* remained unused in Florence, along with the *Victory* and perhaps the *Crouching Youth* and various models, sketches, studies and blocks of marble. When Michelangelo died, his nephew, Leonardo Buonarroti gave the *Slaves* to Cosimo I de' Medici, whose son, Francesco I had them placed in the Large Grotto in the

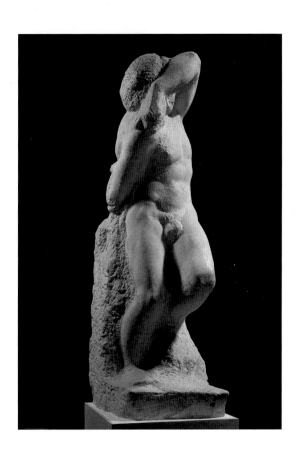

Young Slave,
c. 1520-1532,
marble, height 256 cm;
Florence, Galleria dell'Accademia.

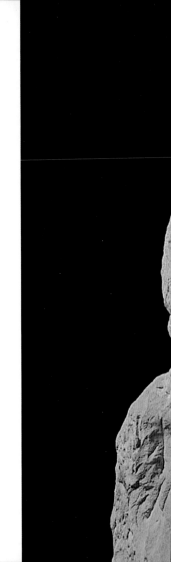

Boboli Gardens that Bernardo Buontalenti was building (1585-1588), between mock mineral incrustations, stalactites and sponges. In 1909 the statues were finally transferred to the Galleria dell'Accademia to lead the way to the Tribune and the *David*.

Owing to their diverse traits and poses the *Slaves* are known as: the *Young Slave,* the *Bearded Slave, Atlas* and the *Awakening Slave.*

Even today, these four statues are astounding for their might and expressive power. The effect is due partly to their incomplete state that exalts the dramatic strength of the four giants imprisoned by the material they seem desperate to escape from. This struggle is rich in symbolism that also recalls the torment to which the "outstanding" artist is subjected as he tries to free the "concept" enclosed in the block. He works tirelessly with his hand "that obeys the intellect" and he models the material by removing the excess to find the shape that corresponds to the Idea (see pages 628-629).

The *Awakening Slave* (1520-1523) quite similar to *Saint Mathew* has crossed legs, in a position more appropriate to a reclining rather than a standing figure and seems to herald the statue of *Dusk* in the Medici Tombs. Another

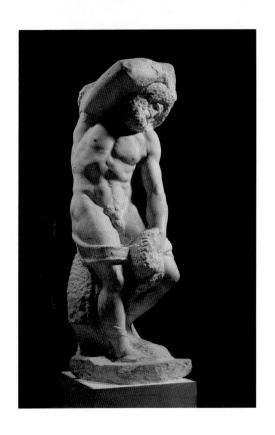

Bearded Slave,
c. 1520-1532,
marble, height 267 cm;
Florence, Galleria dell'Accademia.

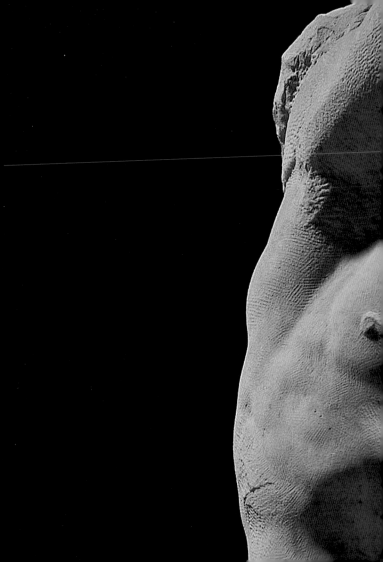

quite similar figure appears in one of Antonio Federighi's relief carvings for the baptismal font of the Siena cathedral.

The *Slaves,* that are bigger than the *Slaves* in the Louvre, still have the shape of the marble blocks from which they are only partially carved. On the *Atlas* we can still see the marks Michelangelo made on the block at the quarry: the three circles he used as a signature, the initial "L" for Leone the name of the quarryman, a boat and a trident. Thus, the four statues make it possible to reconstruct the artist's procedure. He tackled the parallelepiped from one side and only that side, "biting" into the material with his chisel, allowing the shapes to come forth. Vasari gives a literary image in his biography when he compares Michelangelo's technique to a body in a pool of water that slowly, gradually comes out as the water drains off. We can see this when we compare the *Atlas* with the *Bearded Slave.*

Atlas,
c. 1520-1532,
marble, height 277 cm;
Florence, Galleria dell'Accademia.

Their poses are similar to telamons and they seem to be very closely related to the architectural setting where they were to have stood. The *Atlas* and the *Awakening Slave* seem to have been destined for a corner position on the monument since one is carved on two sides and the other starts from a corner of the marble block.

The artist's care in carving the *Slaves* seems to have been devoted mainly to the expanded and contracted torso, tense and in motion; it is what determines the positions of the limbs (with the hands and feet still imprisoned in the stone), while the head and facial features are of secondary interest and seem to remain indistinct to the last.

Awakening Slave,
c. 1520-1532,
marble, height 267 cm;
Florence, Galleria dell'Accademia.

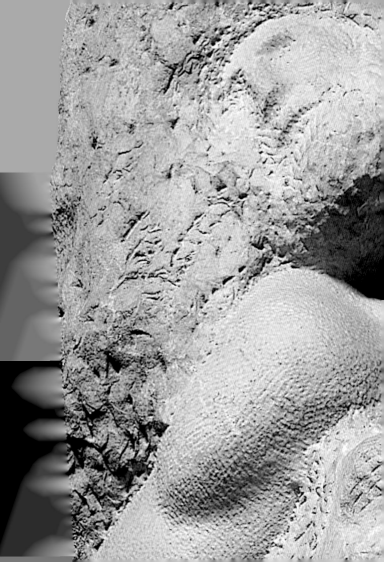

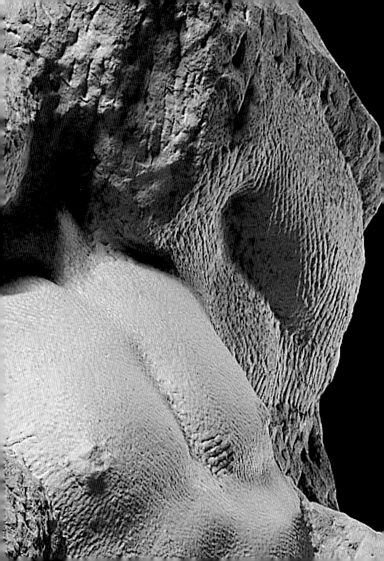

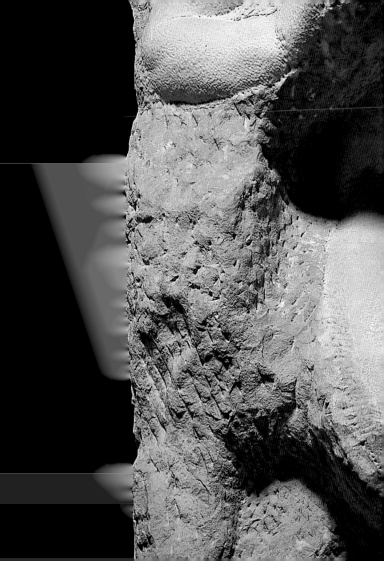

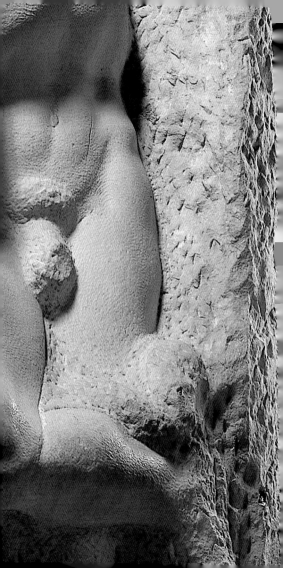

Two Wrestlers

This small clay statue is one of the models Michelangelo made along with sketches and compositional studies to develop formal and static solutions and views of a piece. It depicts two, powerful nude men wrestling. One is erect and holds the other, crouching between his legs; with one hand he grips his adversary's neck and prepares to strike the final blow with the other (the entire arm that should have been behind his shoulders is missing). The group is designed to be admired fully from several viewpoints: in fact, the two bodies are rotated in opposite directions creating a solid yet dynamic whole with upward motion along divergent diagonals.

The destination of this model is still uncertain. In 1928 Johannes Wilde who recomposed the fragments of a

Two Wrestlers,
c. 1525-1530,
light clay, height 41 cm;
Florence, Casa Buonarroti.

sculpture found in Casa Buonarroti said that it was the model for a *Victory* for the Monument to Julius II, along with the group now in Palazzo Vecchio (see pages 342-349). This proposal was accepted by a majority of the critics even in spite of another hypothesis that had it as part of the design for the *Hercules and Cacus* for Piazza della Signoria, that was commissioned during the republican period, revised and transformed several times, but never executed. In 1534 the commission was given to Baccio Bandinelli who carved the group which still stands in front of Palazzo Vecchio.

VICTORY

This sculptural group depicting an allegory of *Victory* was carved in Florence for the Monument to Julius II. In fact, the victor stands over the prostrate defeated figure on the ground; on his head he wears a crown of oak leaves, the heraldic symbol of the Della Rovere family. The ideal and heroic beauty of the slim youth who proudly asserts himself in his nudity in a springing and "serpentine" pose offsets the humiliated, bent figure of the old, conquered bearded man who resembles a barbarian. The mostly polished surface of the victor contrasts with the roughness of the vanquished, with its evident chisel marks.

From the first designs, dated 1505, the bottom register of the tomb was to have had a series of niches, each with a

Victory,
c. 1530-1534,
marble, height 261 cm;
Florence, Palazzo Vecchio, Salone dei Cinquecento.

Victory alternating with a *Slave* resting on the outer pillars and corners. The *Victories* were initially envisioned as females, but in the 1532 contract they were conceived as wrestlers. In light of the relationship with the Monument to Julius II, the allegory was interpreted as the triumph of Victory over one of the provinces conquered by the Church, but it was also interpreted as a tribute to the beauty of Tommaso de' Cavalieri the friend Michelangelo met during that period. In his sculpture the artist returned to themes he had already developed in other statues, such as the youthful face that is quite similar to *Giuliano de' Medici* in the New Sacristy, while the position of the arm recalls the *David*.

After Michelangelo's departure for Rome the sculpture remained in the Via Mozza studio for thirty years until 1564. After the artist's death, his nephew, Leonardo Buonarroti, gave it to Cosimo I de' Medici along with the

Slaves. It was Vasari's idea to place the statue in the Salone dei Cinquecento in Palazzo Vecchio, the main showplace of the Medici dukes that had been remodeled and was being redecorated by Vasari himself. The *Victory* was added to a group of statues against the wall which exalted the triumph of Good, incarnated by the duke, over Evil, represented by the enemies of the Medici state. Furthermore, with his helpers, Giorgio was frescoing the great hall with scenes of battles celebrating Florentine and Medici victories. In this context Michelangelo's statue was given the name with which it is known today, the *Spirit of Victory*.

BRUTUS

The statue is depiction of *Brutus*, Julius Caesar's adopted son who joined the conspiracy to assassinate him in the name of freedom. Michelangelo carved the bust – the only one of his career it seems – for Cardinal Niccolò Ridolfi. The cardinal was an exiled Florentine with strong anti-Medici feelings like his secretary, the scholar Donato Giannotti who acted as intermediary for the commission and is portrayed on the brooch fastening the draped cloth on *Brutus'* shoulder. The piece was conceived in the world of the Florentine exiles in Rome: merchants, bankers, high prelates and scholars, who considered Lorenzino de' Medici – who assassinated the brutal Alessandro dei Medici, the first duke of Florence, in 1537 – a liberating tyrant killer, the "Tuscan Brutus." Michelangelo certainly shared these feelings: when the Florentine Republic was besieged by the papal and imperial troops (1529-1539) he was in charge of the city's defenses. Alessandro's murder triggered interesting disputes on the topic of tyrannicide and its legitimacy among those who had supported the republic and now considered Lorenzino a hero (even though it is more likely that he was just an unknowing pawn in a much vaster game plan drawn up by his cousin, Cosimo I who took his place as duke). The statue may have been carved shortly after Giannotti entered the cardinal's service in 1539 or following Lorenzino's murder in Venice in 1547. Michelangelo turned the unfinished bust over to his pupil Tiberio Calcagni

Brutus,
c. 1539-1548,
marble, height 74 cm;
Florence, Museo Nazionale del Bargello.

who completed the draping. Ferdinando I de' Medici purchased it in 1590 and had it placed in the Uffizi along with an inscription that obscures the statue's political and commemorative purposes: "DVM BRUTI EFFIGIEM SCVLPTOR DE MAMRMORE DVCIT / IN MENTEM SCELERIS VENIT ET ABSTINVIT" ("While the sculptor was carving the marble effigy he remember the crime and stopped").

Compared to Renaissance busts that are much more static, Michelangelo opted for a solution that gives the subject a powerful expression, taking his inspiration from the *Portrait of Caracalla* in the Museo Archeologico in Naples. The observer's gaze is definitely drawn to the seemingly sudden movement of the head. The profile highlights the power of the neck, jaws, the indistinct curly hair. The narrow, parallel grooves made by the gradine construct the face in geometric planes while the aggressive chisel marks of the roughing that are clearly visible create an indistinct and thick mass of hair. Moving to the side we discover the facial features, the bold expression, the strong nose, and tightly closed lips even if the subject's physiognomy is barely developed, reminding us of the fact that Michelangelo was not interested in portraits.

Rachel and Leah

It was in the fifth decade of the XVI century that Michelangelo finally completed the Monument to Julius II. Up to then it had been an immense source of problems and second thoughts due to the ongoing demands from the heirs that he complete it or return the advances he had received with interest. In 1542 he signed a new agreement calling for the erection of a wall tomb in San Pietro in Vincoli (and no longer in Saint Peter's Basilica), with six statues, three of which were to be done by Michelangelo's hand and the others by a trusted assistant working to the master's model.

The three autograph sculptures were *Moses*, (see pages 232-243) the two *Slaves* now in the Louvre (see pages 220-231), and all were made under the 1513 contract and then left in the studio at Macel de' Corvi. Michelangelo assigned Raffaello da Montelupo to make the other three, a *Madonna and Child*, a *Prophet* and a *Sibyl* with a contract dated February 1542.

A few months later, in July, Michelangelo decided to replace the two *Slaves* with two new pieces: *Rachel and Leah*, Old Testament figures, sisters of highly different character who had both been the wife of Jacob. They depict the allegories of the *Contemplative Life* and the *Active Life*. The *Contemplative Life* is beautiful with a veil looking heavenward in prayer. The *Active Life* is a young woman looking into a mirror in her right hand, while in the left she holds a wreath of flowers. The serious and

Rachel or *The Contemplative Life*,
1542-1545,
marble, height 197 cm; Rome,
San Pietro in Vincoli, Monument to Julius II.

succinct definition of the two figures denotes yet another phase in the development of Michelangelo's style and poetics.

The six statues were installed in 1545. And then, the reclining statue of the pope, that Vasari (1568) attributes to Tommaso Boscoli to a design by Michelangelo was placed on top. However, during a recent restoration of the entire monument, Antonio Forcellino has supported the thesis that it is, indeed, an autograph work by Michelangelo (2003).

With the completion of the Monument to Julius II the "tragedy of the burial" as Buonarroti himself called it finally came to an end in 1547. It had been started over forty years before, in 1505. The artist gave the two unused statues, the *Rebellious Slave* and the *Dying Slave* to Roberto Strozzi in exile in Lyon, who had them taken to France in 1550.

Leah or *The Active Life*,
1542-1545,
marble, height 209 cm; Rome,
San Pietro in Vincoli, Monument to Julius II.

BANDINI PIETÀ

Between 1550 and 1555 Michelangelo worked on the *Bandini Pietà* with the idea of having it placed on his own tomb. But, when he had already gotten quite far along, he rejected it because of a flaw in the marble that had come to light. Indeed, overcome by anger he tried to destroy it by hitting it in several points (Vasari 1568). In 1561 Francesco Bandini purchased the piece (hence its current title) and gave it to Tiberio Calcagni for repairs. He fixed some of the broken parts such as the left arm of the Christ and finished others, especially the Magdalene, but he could do nothing to remedy Jesus' broken right leg which is still missing. The statue remained in Bandini's garden at Montecavallo and Vasari vainly tried to have it brought to Florence to use on the tomb he had to build for Michelangelo in Santa Croce. The sculpture finally reached Florence at the end of the XVII century through the offices of Cosimo III de' Medici and was placed in the crypt in San Lorenzo and was later (1722) moved to Santa Maria del Fiore.

Bandini Pietà,
c. 1550-1555,
marble, height 226 cm;
Florence, Museo dell'Opera del Duomo.

This is one of Michelangelo's most moving works, the fruit of the personal involvement of the seventy year old artist with a subject that had always fascinated him. Now, reaching the end of his life it prompted him to renewed and tormented contemplation of grief, the sacrifice of Christ and his salvation that we can also see in his writings. The composition combines elements from the *Pietà* with others from the *Deposition* and the *Entombment*. As opposed to the early *Vatican Pietà* (see pages 150-163) in which, according to the traditional iconography, Christ is on his mother's lap, the *Bandini Pietà* is based on a Flemish model, also used in Florentine paintings (Angelico) in which the body of Christ is in the center, supported in an erect or seated position by two figures, usually the Virgin Mary and Saint John.

Starting from an enormous, single block of marble the artist created a compact group of four figures that come together in a pyramid. The apex is the hooded figure supporting Jesus, probably Nicodemus, the converted Pharisee who in the *Gospel According to John* anoints the Redeemer's body before the burial (even though, it may also have been Joseph of Arimathea). According to Vasari (1568) Michelangelo carved his self-portrait into that figure, confirming how profoundly he projected himself into the sculpture. The fulcrum of the entire composition is the polished body of Christ, with lifeless limbs, sliding downwards. He is bigger than the other figures and his weight seems as unbearable as the grief of the one holding him. The Magdalene is on the left, in a position that separates her from the others, while the Virgin behind the Son holds Him closely burying her face in His hair, in loving contact. Michelangelo designed the composition to give utmost visibility to his Christ, as opposed to the *Vatican Pietà* in which it is only partly visible.

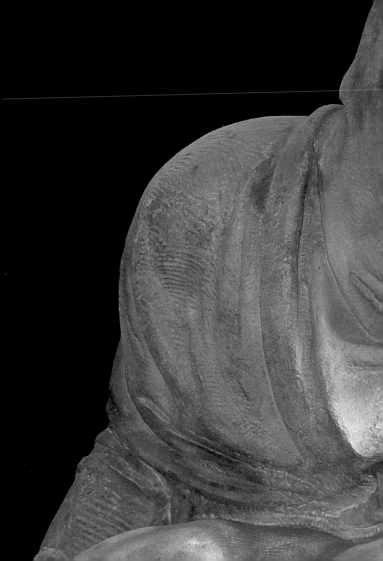

RONDANINI PIETÀ

The *Rondanini Pietà* is the "started statue of a Christ and another figure above, attached to each other, roughed and not finished." as listed in the inventory of Michelangelo's assets found at Macel de' Corvi in Rome after his death (1564). In a letter dated 12 February 1564 from Daniele da Volterra we learn that up to a week before his death Michelangelo was working on a *Pietà* that could not have been other than this one. Its name comes from the Rondanini family which owned the statue for many years in the XIX century.

Rondanini Pietà,
c. 1552-1564,
marble, height 195 cm;
Milan, Castello Sforzesco.

The slenderness and spirituality of the figures has been often emphasized; perhaps the artist had found an effective example in Medieval and especially Gothic statuary. The sculpture is the fruit of several transformations Michelangelo had made on the theme of the *Pietà* from a first plan with a powerful Christ supported by one or more figures (similar to the *Bandini Pietà*) to a second version with an emaciated Christ held by only one figure, the Virgin Mary. In the foreground we can see part of a naked arm with powerful muscles, hanging down which, in all likelihood is from first version of the Christ and probably was to have been eliminated, just like His legs that are totally foreign to the final, fragile body. As he worked on the modified version Michelangelo cut away the already carved marble working with his chisel from the front to outline the body of the Son that is practically sunken into the mother. The new head was carved from the right shoulder of the earlier figure behind him (perhaps a Nicodemus as in the *Bandini Pietà*), while the arms were carved out of the hips and legs. From the chest came the hands and arms of the Virgin Mary holding Jesus. Here we can see traces of the original figure: facial features in the veil and a naked leg.

A few years ago, during excavations near a wall adjacent to the church of Santa Maria in Trastevere in Rome, a head of a Christ with part of a shoulder was found that some critics maintain as belonging to the first version of the *Rondanini Pietà*. However, the fragmentary state of the piece does not permit any definitive attribution.

With its silent and allusive mysticism and the dramatic intensity expressed in the slender, tired bodies the *Rondanini Pietà* is the utmost embodiment of the elderly artist's spirituality and his inexhaustible creative strength.

CRUCIFIX

From some letters to Leonardo Buonarroti, Michelangelo's nephew, signed by Lorenzo Mariottini and Tiberio Calcagni in 1562, we know that the artist wanted to carve a wooden Crucifix and was waiting for the tools that he had specifically ordered from Florence. In July 1563, a few months before he died, Michelangelo was working on the Crucifix that he probably wanted to give to his nephew. The piece, mentioned in the sources, is associated with a small wooden model in Casa Buonarroti and several late drawings of the *Crucifixion* (now in London, Paris, Windsor and Oxford).

There is no documentary proof supporting the identification of the Crucifix mentioned in the letter with the sculpture in Casa Buonarroti. But it is certain that the carving – and Michelangelo's autograph is widely acknowledged – and definitely dates from the final years of his life. Indeed, in this wooden *Crucifix* the powerful, albeit small forms, the essential and allusive shapes, the rough, vibrant surface where we can clearly see the gouge marks are elements that recall the intense spirituality in the works of the almost ninety-year old artist who had become engrossed in an agonizing inner monologue on the themes of death, suffering, the sacrifice of Christ and the Resurrection.

Crucifix,
c. 1562-1563,
wood, height 27 cm;
Florence, Casa Buonarroti.

porticu

Architecture

Michelangelo began his career as an architect only after the deaths of Pope Julius II in 1513 and Bramante the following year. In fact, the commission for the Monument to Julius II had been blocked several times by the patron himself. Michelangelo's opportunity came with election of the Medici pope, Leo X (1513-1521) who sent the artist to Florence to complete the Fabbrica di San Lorenzo, the Medici family's church. The next Medici pope, Clement VII (1523-1534), confirmed Michelangelo's appointment in spite of the interval of the second Republic (1527-1530) when the artist – having abandoned his Medici commissions – was in charge of strengthening the city's fortifications against the siege by the imperial and pontifical armies. In Rome Michelangelo had the opportunity to prove himself as an architect after the deaths of Raphael and Antonio da Sangallo, close followers of Bramante. Only after Sangallo died in 1546 was Michelangelo appointed architect of the Fabbrica di San Pietro.

Such late acknowledgement can only be explained by the fact that his innovative style caused "embarrassment." It broke away from all the classical rules, and aimed at creating dynamic structures, finely modeled shapes and dialectical compositions.

Plans for the Church of San Giovanni
dei Fiorentini in Rome, c. 1559;
Florence, Casa Buonarroti, inv. 121A.

Chapel of Leo X
in Castel Sant'Angelo

Giovanni de' Medici, son of Lorenzo the Magnificent was elected Pope Leo X in 1513. At the time Michelangelo was in Rome working on the Monument to Pope Julius II. Leo X commissioned him to build a chapel in the courtyard of Castel Sant'Angelo that would be dedicated to Cosmas and Damian, the Medici family's patron saints. This chapel is considered Michelangelo's first architectural endeavor. Situated in the delle Palle Courtyard, it was built under the supervision of Antonio da Sangallo the Younger. Inside are the Medici devices and outside those of the Pope, that is the lion's head and ring with three feathers. Michelangelo's façade covers the right wall of the chapel. Mentioned in documents as early as 1535 it clearly reflects Michelangelo's style of that period even though Sangallo, who built it, added two lateral niches that modified the original proportions. Michelangelo used marble for this wall decoration, as he did for other designs dating from this period, such as the Monument to Julius II or the façade of San Lorenzo in Florence. The central span has a pediment and projects forward with respect to the sides. In the center, the broad aperture is divided into four parts, reminiscent of ancient, cross-shaped Roman windows, however, they have additional elements of great plasticity that already reveal the beginning of Michelangelo's original vision.

Chapel of Leo X,
c. 1514;
Rome, Castel Sant'Angelo.

Kneeling Windows, Palazzo Medici

While he was busy with the façade of San Lorenzo, Michelangelo "… made at that time for the Palace of the Medici a model for the knee-shaped windows of those rooms that are at the corner" (Vasari 1568). Lorenzo de' Medici, Duke of Urbino, son of Piero the Unfortunate and nephew of the pope, wanted to close off the corner loggia of the palace that opened onto the intersection of Via Larga (now Via Cavour) and Via de' Gori, and thus create another room on the ground floor.

The two windows were built in 1517, in the portion of wall that closed the respective arches of the loggia. They were fitted with "jalousies of perforated copper, which are certainly admirable things" (Vasari), that were crafted by the goldsmith Piloto under Michelangelo's supervision. This solution eliminated the close relationship between the interior of the palace and the surrounding urban context that had distinguished the XV century building. The windows Michelangelo designed were totally innovative because of their proportions, the vertical projection onto the street, the classical notes in the fronton and mainly the scrolls that add a dynamic, plastic note to the structure. This type of window soon became popular and was used on other Florentine palazzos in the following decades.

"Kneeling" Windows,
1517;
Florence, Palazzo Medici Riccardi.

Church of San Lorenzo, Façade

When the son of Lorenzo the Magnificent visited Florence in 1515, two years after his election to the papacy as Leo X, he revived his interest the still incomplete Medici *fabbriche*. Among these was the Renaissance church of San Lorenzo designed by Brunelleschi a century earlier. It was just a short distance from the Palazzo Medici and was under the patronage of the family that had its tombs there.

Between the end of 1515 and the beginning of 1516, Leo X decided to sponsor the construction of the church façade on the still rough masonry. He asked the best architects to submit drawings and models. In addition to Michelangelo the competitors included Baccio d'Agnolo, Giuliano and Antonio Sangallo the Elder, Andrea and Jacopo Sansovino and Raphael.

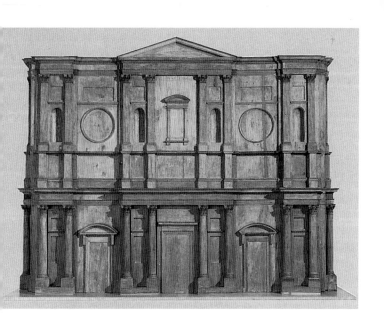

Model for the façade of San Lorenzo,
c. 1518,
wood, 216 x 283 x 50 cm;
Florence, Casa Buonarroti inv. 518.

After a close contest Buonarroti was awarded the entire commission – for both the architecture and sculptural decorations and finally signed the contract alone on 19 January 1518. The wooden model, now in Casa Buonarroti, probably dates from that time. Therefore, it would be the final version approved by the pope and reflects the third of the three plans, documented by just as many drawings in Casa Buonarroti (nn. 45A, 47A and 43A).

The façade Michelangelo envisioned seems like that of a private palazzo or public building, concealing the traditional three-part structure of the church built to a basilica plan. The artist had developed a unitary solution that made it possible to use the classical orders with skilful balance. The structure, with a close network of horizontal and vertical members has a plastic and dynamic look that was unusual for the Florence of the era.

From December 1516 to the autumn of 1519 Michelangelo lived at Carrara, Pietrasanta and Serravezza to supervise the quarrying of the marble. But, on 10 March 1520 Leo X relieved him of all his obligations. The materials procured up to then were used for cathedral floor. Work on the San Lorenzo façade continued at a slower pace for a while and then came to a complete halt upon the death of Leo X in 1521.

First plan for the façade of San Lorenzo,
1516; Florence,
Casa Buonarroti inv. 45A.

TRIBUNE OF THE RELICS
IN SAN LORENZO

On 14 October 1525 Pope Clement VII asked Michelangelo to design a ciborium for the choir of the church of San Lorenzo. It was to hold the church's precious relics, most of which came from the collection of Lorenzo the Magnificent. The ciborium was to have been made of stone and supported by ancient porphyry columns found in Rome. However, Michelangelo proposed a tribune or loggia on the inside wall of the church centered above the entrance door.

Notwithstanding doubts about the high position of the relics the pope accepted the concept of the balcony in 1531. The relics were placed in the new balcony in December 1532 and Clement VII complimented Michelangelo a few months later.

Tribune of the Relics,
1531-1532;
Florence, San Lorenzo

New Sacristy in San Lorenzo

In 1519, via his cousin Cardinal Giulio de' Medici, Pope Leo X asked Michelangelo to build the new sacristy next to the right transept of the church of San Lorenzo. It was to be a mausoleum to house the tombs of four of the patron's family members: Lorenzo and Giuliano, the Magnificent, fathers of Leo X and Giulio, respectively and their recently deceased namesakes, Lorenzo Duke of Urbino and Giuliano Duke of Nemours (for more information see the chapter on Sculpture pages 250-303), Michelangelo began work in 1520 and carried on with several interruptions and slowdowns until 1534 when he left for Rome.

The architectural layout of the chapel was inspired by Brunelleschi's Old Sacristy built a century earlier in the left transept. It consists of two square rooms surmounted by a dome; the bigger of the two houses the tombs, the smaller one has an altar. Michelangelo also used the same dimensions, materials and colors – grey and white – as Brunelleschi. But in the larger of the rooms, even though he used *pietra serena* for the framework extending it to the corner pilaster strip, at the bottom he used white stucco with a fine marble cladding that forms a dynamic series of niches and cornices.

Furthermore, to accentuate the verticality he added an intermediate register between the walls and the impost of the dome. The trapezoidal windows up above, with the curved tympanums that seem to accompany arches supporting the dome further enhance the effect. This solution was inspired by the Pantheon, with the ceiling panels arranged in rays concluding the upward pattern in the lantern above where light shines in intensely and then spreads evenly throughout the space.

The marble cladding of the bottom register with the tombs of the two dukes was surprising to contemporaries and became an essential model for Florentine Mannerist architecture. According to Vasari (1568), in the Medici Chapel Michelangelo, "made in it an ornamentation in a composite order, in a more varied and more original manner than any other master at any time, whether ancient or modern, had been able to achieve": aediculae, trabeations, capitals, bases, doors and sarcophagi were not classifiable in the classical architectural orders. The New Sacristy broke the bonds with famous models from the past and opened the doors to freedom and new ideas.

On pages 396-397,
New Sacristy,
1519-1534;
Florence, San Lorenzo.

Laurentian Library

While he was monitoring progress of the work on the New Sacristy, shortly after his election to the papacy as Clement VII on 1523, the former Giulio de' Medici asked Michelangelo to build a library within the San Lorenzo complex to store the Medici collections of codexes and manuscripts. The priceless collection, once housed in the palace on Via Larga had been requisitioned by the Republic in 1494, and made part of the San Marco Library. In 1508 Cardinal Giovanni de' Medici (later Pope Leo X) "redeemed" the collection for money and took it to Rome, while awaiting suitable premises in Florence. Michelangelo carefully drew up the plans for the Laurentian Library, from the architecture to the ceiling to the desks. He launched the work in 1524, but in 1534, having obtained the pope's permission to return to Rome, he left it unfinished. The work was finally completed by Niccolò Tribolo, Giorgio Vasari and Bartolomeo Ammannati under the reign of Cosimo I, between 1548 and 1571 (when it was opened). The same three also finished the New Sacristy working to the drawings and scanty information left by the master.

The whole, which is one of the finest and unitary examples of XVI century architecture, consists of two rooms, the vestibule and the reading room. From the shadows of the vestibule characterized by strong dynamic tension, up along the splendid, semi-curving staircase we come to the long, rectangular room flooded by light that

Laurentian Library,
Reading Room, 1524-1571;
Florence, San Lorenzo complex.

shines in through the windows decorated with grotesques, Medici devices and coats of arms. The sunlight exalts the warm tones of the *cotto* floor and the wooden furnishings and ceiling, creating a soothing emotional and intellectual effect. In a play of traditional gray and white, the architecture of the vestibule soars upwards thanks to the energetic plastic interplay of the surfaces with their paired scrolls and columns, cornices, niches, and alternating tympanums. The looming tension of the walls relaxes in the waving rhythm of the staircase built by Ammannati in 1559 to a terracotta model by Michelangelo. Divided into three flights in the first section, the steps are straight on the sides and curved in the middle, flowing into the final elliptical group. A monumental doorway leads to the reading room where the emphasis becomes horizontal contrasting the verticality of the vestibule. Here, all the languages of different techniques work together in expressing a single formal concept. We see this in the way the wooden ceiling carvings by Giovan Battista del Tasso and Carota harmonize with the white patterns on the *cotto* floor made by Santi Buglioli.

Laurentian Library,
Vestibule, 1524-1571;
Florence, San Lorenzo complex.

THE MONUMENT TO JULIUS II

Michelangelo completed the monument to the Della Rovere pope, Julius II, in February 1545. Actually, it is a cenotaph since the pontiff – who died in 1513 – was buried in the Grotte Vaticane. Finally, the "tragedy of the tomb" as he had called it came to an end after forty tormented years. It all began in 1505, when he signed the first contract with the pope for an immense four-sided, free-standing monument with forty colossal statues to be placed in Saint Peter's Basilica. There followed new contracts and modifications to the plans, first requested by the pope, then by his heirs who wanted to reduce both the size of the monument and the number of statues, forcing Michelangelo to set aside huge sculptures that he had already begun (see entries on *Slaves* in the Louvre, pages 220-231, and in the Accademia, pages 318-335). Finally, the marble structure with the statuary was finally mounted between 1542 and 1545. Some of the statues are by Michelangelo (*Moses, Rachel* and *Leah*), others by his helpers (the *Virgin and Child* at the top and the *Prophets* at the sides, with *Julius II* in the center, were carved by Tommaso Boscoli, probably to a model by Michelangelo). The construction of the monument, done by stone-cutters and carvers reflects the long and complex gestation of the project. The lower register reveals a style datable around the 1520-1530s. It has classical decorative elements such as candelabra-type pilaster strips and parts similar to his earlier works such as the

scrolls on plinths resembling those in the vestibule of the Laurentian library, or the cloaked *Terms* reminiscent of the *Captives* originally intended for the monument. The upper register, elongated to match the arch, reveals an austere and simplified, subdued architectural language lacking in decoration (except for the herm) which reflects a later cultural context.

On the whole, it presents contradictions that were also noticed by contemporaries including Michelangelo's biographer, Ascanio Condivi (1553), who defined it as "patched up and redone." To which the artist replied in a letter "If everything that is patched up looked like this!"

A major restoration of the entire monument was completed in 2003. It provided an opportunity to retrace its difficult and controversial history and to reconsider Michelangelo's autography of its various parts. As to the structure on the whole, it acquired a lighter, more even tone. The XVIII century lunette, that reduced the light coming from behind the monument, was removed, and the rectangular apertures were recovered, by removing their windows.

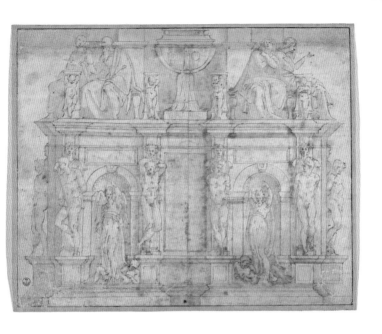

On page 405:
Monument to Julius II,
1542-1545, marble;
Rome, San Pietro in Vincoli.

Plan for the Monument to Julius II,
1505 or 1513;
Florence, Gabinetto Disegni
e Stampe degli Uffizi, inv. 68 Er.

PIAZZALE OF THE CAPITOLINE HILL

Michelangelo's design for the arrangement of the piazzale or square on the Capitoline Hill was part of the "urban renewal plan" ordered by Pope Paul III (1534-1549). The ideal center of Ancient Rome, the hill was traditionally the seat of the Roman government, the senators and conservators, the elected magistrates who lived there.

The Palazzo Senatorio, facing the Forum, had been built in the XII century and modified during the Renaissance. The Palazzo dei Conservatori was built in the XV century opposite the XII century church of Santa Maria in Aracoeli. The equestrian statue of Marcus Aurelius was moved to the Capitoline Piazzale from the Lateran palace by order of the pope in 1538.

Michelangelo prepared a general outline plan perhaps as early as 1537 and then, according to his method, dealt with the individual issues one at a time. Vasari talks about Michelangelo's work in the second edition of the *Lives* (1568); other sources, engravings by XVI century artists, give us an idea of the artist's innovative concepts. The same architectural unity of the plaza and the buildings depose in favor of Michelangelo as does the certain autography of the base of the equestrian statue. In addition, Michelangelo designed the stairs of the Palazzo Senatorio, the stairs leading to the piazza and some of the arches of the Palazzo dei Conservatori, all documented by the artist between 1544 and 1564. This terrace overlooking the city became the ideal link with the imposing new

Piazzale of the Capitoline Hill,
1538-1564;
Rome.

Saint Peter's Basilica. In the middle, the driving force is the statue of Marcus Aurelius that determines the perspective lines of the oblique fronts of the two lateral palazzos and the pattern of the pavement. Thus a twelve-pointed star of gray and white stones radiates from the base of the statue. Michelangelo also designed the new façade for the Palazzo Senatorio that was actually completed in the XVII century by Girolamo Rainaldi who took over from Giacomo della Porta in 1602. The Palazzo Nuovo Buonarroti had designed as an indispensable complement was to have been a symmetrical copy of the Palazzo dei Conservatori; it was only begun in 1604 and completed by Rainaldi in 1654. On the façades of these buildings Michelangelo used gigantic pilaster strips that are horizontally balanced by the cornice, trabeations and friezes.

SAINT PETER'S BASILICA AND THE DOME

With the advent of Pope Julius II, the reconstruction of Saint Peter's Basilica became a reality. Work was begun under Donato Bramante, calling for a Greek Cross plan with projecting apses; the hemispherical dome in the middle was to be raised in steps on a drum surrounded by columns. Bramante died in 1514, and Raphael was appointed to succeed him as official architect of the Fabbrica (1515). The Pope ordered that the structure be replaced with a longitudinal plan. Bearing in mind the already existing parts, an elongated section was "grafted" onto the central. After Raphael died in 1520 the work was continued by Antonio da Sangallo the Younger, flanked by Baldassare Peruzzi. After work resumed – it had been interrupted by the Sack of Rome (1527) – Pope Paul III gave new drive to construction and in 1546, when Sangallo died, he appointed Michelangelo as chief architect. This project occupied the final years of the artist's life. He accepted the appointment under the condition that he be fully in charge and responsible for the work and not receive any payment since he considered the assignment a way of atoning for his sins.

He courageously threw out the design, and decided to return to the original concept with a central plan. The wooden model he made that had been approved by the pope has been lost.

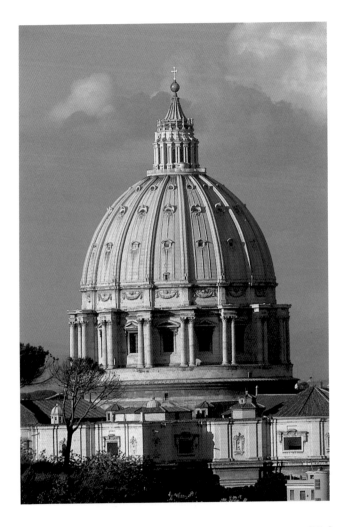

Michelangelo began by reinforcing the external pillars built by Bramante, he created the semicircular apses on the north and south, completed the bottom cornice of the drum, also preparing the first of the semi-domes in the south transept (Chapel of the King of France) and started work on the tambour, or drum, of the dome in 1554. With a minimum number of changes he was able to restore unity and compactness to the design. When the works were interrupted from 1556 to 1661 the now eighty-year old Michelangelo decided to build a linden wood model of the drum and dome to a scale of 1:15 where each internal and external structural detail could be seen. The dome, inspired by the Florence cathedral, comprised two hemispheric vaults; the outer now with a raised arch was probably modified during the pontificate of Sixtus V. The ribbing on Michelangelo's dome projected further outward, like the pilaster strips and cornice of the drum, and finally the lantern he designed was slimmer than the one built by Giacomo della Porta.

On page 413:
Saint Peter's dome,
1546-1564;
Vatican City.

PALAZZO FARNESE

The palace was built by Cardinal Alessandro Farnese who became Pope Paul III in 1534. The initial work was done under the direction of Antonio da Sangallo the Younger, who followed the traditional canons for patrician homes in the city: a two story palace with an inner courtyard with three orders.

When Sangallo died in 1546 Michelangelo inherited the project which was already well along. Therefore, it is likely that he accepted it for the pure pleasure of making changes to what had been done by his detested rival. The changes began with the construction of the imposing cornice on the main façade that was raised by about one meter; then came the large window above the door, surmounted by the huge coat of arms. Michelangelo also designed the courtyard, the ionic frieze above the *piano nobile,* the mezzanine, and the entire order of the second floor characterized by its original windows.

Michelangelo did not complete the courtyard; when the pope died work was continued under Vignola who did not follow Buonarroti's plans.

Palazzo Farnese,
1546-1549;
Rome.

Sforza Chapel
in Santa Maria Maggiore

The Sforza Chapel is situated in the left nave of the basilica. Vasari (1568) tells us that Guido Ascano Sforza, the arch-priest of Santa Maria Maggiore commissioned Michelangelo to build it. However, it was Tiberio Calcagni who took over, on request of the old and tired Michelangelo. The chapel was still unfinished when both Michelangelo and Calcagni died, so it was completed by Giacomo della Porta in 1573. Therefore all the construction work was done after Michelangelo's death. This explains the inconsistencies and the lack of care.

The chapel is independent of the basilica and until the XVIII century "restoration" it had a façade that does not seem to have been by Michelangelo. The interior, however, perfectly reflects his central plan architecture. The system for supporting the vault on four columns that airily soar above the walls, and the bare masonry framework are clearly traceable to the artist. Given the many changes made over the centuries, the drawings conserved in Casa Buonarroti in Florence and in the British Museum in London are of utmost importance as they illustrate the evolution of Michelangelo's ideas for both the perspective and the plan.

Sforza Chapel,
c. 1560;
Rome, Basilica of Santa Maria Maggiore.

Santa Maria degli Angeli

The church inside the Baths of Diocletian is Michelangelo's last great architectural project. Appointed by Pope Pius IV to build a church in the ancient Roman structure, the artist turned to what today would be called "minimalism." The church was to complement the ancient structure and not traumatize it. The alterations done to the church over the centuries have significantly modified Michelangelo's design which is barely discernible. He wanted the church to encompass the large *tepidarium* and the small adjacent rooms, the rotunda leading to the *calidarium* and the swimming pool which was to become a rectangular choir with a barrel vault, enclosed by a semicircular apse. The church could be accessed, via the existing entrance and a door located at the end of what is now the transept, creating a T-shaped crossing. The Roman granite columns supported plastered vaults that are now covered by XVIII century trabeations. Michelangelo's monumental, yet unadorned design conserved the classical heritage while creating new effects.

Church of Santa Maria degli Angeli,
from 1561;
Rome.

Porta Pia

At the end of 1560 Pope Pius IV decided to build a road that would run straight from the Quirinale to the Aurelian Walls, between the Salaria and Nomentana gates to the city. At the end of his the new road he also decided to built a monumental gate, and name in it his own honor, *Pia*. According to Vasari, Michelangelo submitted three sets of plans to the pope who selected the least expensive. The payment records show Michelangelo's name up to 1565, the year it is believed work was completed. The most interesting features are the portal and the original blind windows. The front, designed by Michelangelo, is a plastic block with even more complex elements such as the curved fronton that breaks inside the tympanum or the striking contrasts between the smooth surface of the central part and the roughness on the sides. The fluted pilaster strips on either side of the portal create a picturesque effect, especially when viewed from a distance – the way the artist preferred. The attic was probably completed after Michelangelo's death, either distorting his original plans or working without the guidance of his drawing; it was destroyed in 1567, perhaps it collapsed and was only rebuilt in 1853. A drawing, conserved in the Casa Buonarroti museum in Florence is probably one of the most interesting he made for the gate: on the same sheet we can see the various solutions that overlap like a live, moving body.

Porta Pia,
1561-1565;
Rome.

On page 424,
Plan for Porta Pia,
c. 1561;
Florence, Casa Buonarroti,
inv. 106 Ar.

On page 425,
Plan for Porta Pia,
c. 1561;
Florence, Casa
Buonarroti, inv. 102 Ar.

Painting

Around 1549, in a letter to Benedetto Varchi, Michelangelo offered his response to the question of the primacy of the arts: "I say that to me the more a painting seems like sculpture the better it is and the more a sculpture looks like a painting the worse it is." With these words the artist clearly revealed his propensity for sculpture, using it as the common denominator for his three arts. In Michelangelesque painting, the human figures grasped in complex motion are associated with a palette of light, abstract and rather sharp colors; they convey the concept of beauty as a reflection of the divine on earth. Although Michelangelo did not do many paintings, some of them are so grandiose and innovative that they were immediately acknowledged as unsurpassable masterpieces. Among the paintings that did not survive is the fresco of the *Battle of Cascina* for the Salone dei Cinquecento in Palazzo Vecchio as the companion to Leonardo's *Battle of Anghiari* – neither of which was ever done (see pages 62-63). Since the cartoon for the *Battle of Cascina* (1506-1508) was lost, Buonarroti's creation can be traced through partial copies and some of his own studies. The cartoon, that was a "school" for young artists, depicted an unusual rendering of heroic humanity driven to action by powerful impulses and captured in "extravagant attitudes" (Vasari 1568).

Ceiling of the Sistine Chapel,
detail of the *Prophet Jeremiah*.

MANCHESTER MADONNA

The attribution of the *Virgin and Child with Saint John and four Angels* in the National Gallery in London to Michelangelo has long been disputed and only relatively recently has become accepted. The painting, is also known as the *Manchester Madonna* for the city where it was first publicly displayed in 1857 with the prestigious attribution to Buonarroti.

Later it was associated with a group of paintings with a Michelangelesque imprint, and attributed to an unknown artist known as the Master of the Manchester Madonna who, because of certain stylist aspects typical of Ferrara, had been proposed as Piero or Pietro d'Argenta. He was Michelangelo's original helper from the village of Argenta near Ferrara and was believed to have used the master's drawings for the London painting.

Virgin and Child with Saint John and four Angels
(*Manchester Madonna*),
c. 1495-1497,
panel, 104.5 x 77 cm;
London, National Gallery.

The Virgin in the center is seated on a throne or chair that is not visible, upon a rustic rocky step; her breast is bare, recalling the iconography of the Madonna of Humility. In her right hand is a book that she tries to hold away from her Son as if to protect Him from His destiny written there. Jesus is determinedly climbing onto her knee, getting a foothold in the folds of her mantle: thus the Virgin becomes *scala coeli* as in the *Madonna of the Stairs* (see pages 110-115). Slightly behind and next to the Virgin the young Saint John, dressed in an animal skin timidly peers out with the fingers of his right hand in a "V" as if to hold the reed cross, his attribute which was not painted. Four standing angels are arranged on the sides of the holy group, standing close together, the ones on the left are slightly more than sketched, while the two on the right are practically finished. With restrained mournfulness they are reading a scroll, perhaps the prophecies given to them by John.

The painting is unfinished. Some parts, such as the angels on the left and Mary's hair, are still drawings on the gesso, while other parts such as the external part of the Virgin's mantle that is darkly shaded and was to have been finished with ultramarine blue or azurite, or the red of her dress and that of the angel are lacking the final layer of color and finishing touches.

Even though it is incomplete, the high quality is evident and its characteristics today – after recent studies and restorations – support the thesis of Michelangelo's autography. The confident arrangement of the figures in the

space, their twisting bodies, especially the Virgin and Saint John, reveal features similar to Michelangelo's earlier sculptures such as the *Bacchus* (Museo Nazionale del Bargello) that he finished in 1497 and the *Bruges Madonna*. In particular, the relationship between the Virgin and the Child in the painting are further developed in the 1506 sculpture (see pages 196-203).

References to Ghirlandaio's style, and especially the figurative solutions used by other XV century Florentine artists such as Luca Della Robbia, Sandro Botticelli, Cosimo Rosselli and Filippino Lippi, keep the *Manchester Madonna* strongly rooted in the Florentine background of its author. Even the painting technique (preparatory pen and ink drawing, green earth preparation of the flesh tones, egg tempera) reflect the late XV century methods of Ghirlandaio's workshop even if the strong blanching effect of the light on the angels' red robes and the notes of sparkling color on the sash of the first angel on the right point to the palette he used in the *Doni Tondo* (see pages 442-455).

On the basis of these comparisons, the *Manchester Madonna* could be dated around 1495-1496 when Michelangelo returned to Florence from Bologna, or – according to Hirst (1994) – the beginning of his Rome sojourn around 1497.

THE ENTOMBMENT

The only one of Michelangelo's paintings today that can be dated between the *Manchester Madonna* and the *Doni Tondo* is the *Entombment* in the National Gallery, London. Hirst (1994) has dated it 1500-1501, that is at the conclusion of the artist's sojourn in Rome. In the XVII century it was in the Farnese collection in Rome. Like the other painting in the National Gallery, this one is also unfinished and very problematic: in the past, it too, had been attributed to the anonymous Master of the Manchester Madonna. Furthermore, the use of oil paint on the tempera created doubts as to Michelangelo's autography because the artist had declared himself "hostile" to that technique. The subject of the painting, evidently made for an altar, portrays great yet restrained tragedy: Christ's body, borne by three, is being led to the tomb amidst the composed sorrow of the pious women and the presence of the Virgin Mary, who is a mere outline in the right foreground. The composition, that presents a front view of Christ between the arms of an elderly Joseph of Arimathea, while a robust John and a woman support him with a cloth that passes beneath his legs, was already traced in earlier depictions of the Pietà by XV century Florentine artists starting with Angelico.

Furthermore, a certain Nordic accent in the expressions recalls the *Entombment* by Rogier van der Weyden that probably belonged to the Medici and is now in the Uffizi.

The Entombment,
c. 1500-1501,
panel, 161.7 x 149.9 cm;
London, National Gallery.

The construction of the group with the vertically suspended Christ continued to interest Michelangelo throughout his life as we can see in the marble *Bandini Pietà* in the Museo dell'Opera del Duomo in Florence, and the *Rondanini Pietà* in Milan. If the slim, youthful body of the Christ recalls the wooden *Crucifix* in Santo Spirito, the pose is a projection of the *Vatican Pietà* viewed from above. The straining figures of the bearers approach the powerful and heroic interpretations of the human body typical of Michelangelo, that is exemplified in the *David* that he began in 1501. Indeed, the Saint John in the painting is the mirror image of a figure in a study for the *David* that is now in the Louvre. And finally Joseph of Arimathea's head seems to anticipate that of Saint Joseph in the *Doni Tondo.* There is still a preparatory drawing, in the Louvre, for the kneeling Magdalene on the left (see page 29); it shows a young nude woman with a long, delicate torso contemplating the crown of thorns in her hand. The crown, however, is missing from the painting.

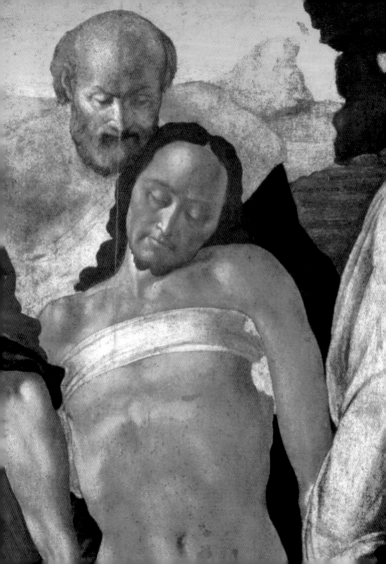

According to Hirst (1994) the painting may have been commissioned by the Augustinian Friars in Rome, according to the last will and testament of the bishop of Crotone, Giovanni Ebu who had wanted a painting in his chapel dedicated to the *Pietà*. The Augustinians paid Michelangelo in advance in 1500, but he went back to Florence the following year, never finished the painting and returned the money to the monks who commissioned Andrea da Venezia to do another. The 1500 dating of the painting reveals a Michelangelo with a mature artistic personality that was also very advanced with respect to his contemporaries, none of whom at that time could have conceived of such a solemn, large painting with its silent, restrained grief.

DONI TONDO

The *Doni Tondo* is the only panel painting that is definitely known to be by Michelangelo. He painted the *Holy Family* for Agnolo Doni and his wife Maddalena (née Strozzi) probably for their wedding on 31 January 1504 or a few years later to celebrate the birth of their first child Maria on 8 September 1507. Raphael, the other great artist of the time painted the couple's portraits during the same period, that is around 1506. The circular painting falls into the most typical XV century Florentine tradition generally used for private homes or the headquarters of the guilds. Famous examples with which Michelangelo was probably familiar are the *Madonna of the Pomegranate* by Botticelli, or Luca Signorelli's *Madonna of Humility* (both in the Uffizi). Michelangelo's debt to the latter is quite evident if not indeed forceful (the Virgin in the foreground, the nudes in the back, the prophets in the frame).

Holy Family (Doni Tondo),
c. 1507,
panel, diameter 120 cm;
Florence, Uffizi.

The composition portrays the grandiose "Holy Family of jugglers" (Longhi 1980). It looks like a painted sculpture, with a marked three-dimensionality, strong plasticity emphasized by the contrast between light and shadow. Firmly placed in the middle of the group the Virgin – who is the absolute protagonist – turns around to hold the Child above her shoulders being handed to her by Saint Joseph. Mary has strong features and is portrayed with bare head and shoulders, with classical garments and a book on her lap. Her features seem to anticipate the Sibyls on the Sistine Chapel ceiling, just as the young nudes in the background recall the ceiling's *Ignudi*. Even the palette, with its light, cold, almost harshly juxtaposed brilliant colors preludes the Sistine chromatics that were recovered in the last restoration. The *Doni Tondo* is one of the primary paintings that opened the XVI century season of the "modern manner" according to Giorgio Vasari's famous definition. It is characterized by the embracing space that dilates in depth, the dynamic composition that moves upwards, the abstract and light colors, the monumentality of the figures, the twisting yet sentimental poses. Precisely those poses and respective attitudes were inspired by Hellenistic models, the antiquities that stimulated such a strong expressive accent in early XVI century visual arts as to mark a turning point. In fact, inspirations have been traced to the *Belvedere Apollo* (the second nude on the left in the background), the *Farnese Hercules,* the *Belvedere Torso,* the so-called *Dying Alexander* (seen here in the Virgin's face and

then in Jonah in the Sistine Chapel), and the *Laocoon* found in Rome in January 1506. It is precisely the reference to the immense sculptural group in the nude on Joseph's right that would confirm the latest dating for the painting as 1507. A tireless student of ancient models, a lively and original interpreter of inspiring subjects, Michelangelo "… had a most tenacious memory; he could remember and make use of the works of others where he had only once seen them…" (Vasari 1568).

The *Doni Tondo* is still in its original frame that was probably designed by Michelangelo himself and perhaps carved by Marco and Francesco del Tasso. Within the decoration of intertwining plants, screaming masks and gryphons with lion heads, are the three crescents, from the Strozzi coat of arms. Five heads also project from the frame: on the sides, two Sibyls and two Prophets announcing the advent of the Savior and at the top, the suffering Christ, the conclusion of His incarnation, the beginning of which is the theme of the painting.

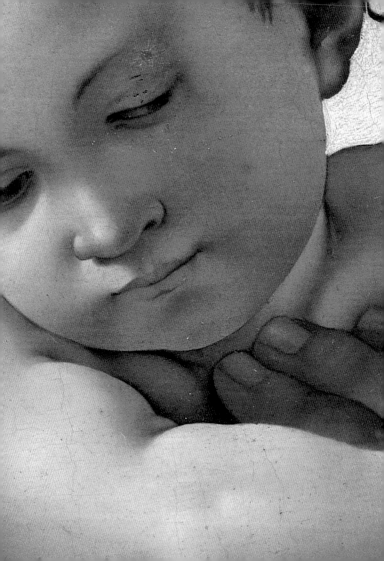

Here, the focus, filled with meanings is Jesus as Joseph hands Him to Mary, it alludes to the transition of human destiny from the house of David to the Universal Church. In the Virgin's expression we can read her awareness of her Son's destiny, that is reiterated by the closed book on her lap. The Holy Family is on a limited ground, almost *hortus conclusus* where sprigs of clover in the foreground allude to the Trinity. Near the stone wall on the right is the young Saint John, venerated by Florentines as the patron saint of the city. The little hermit, the last of the prophets introduces the theme of baptism that is developed in the background, perhaps with reference to Saint Paul's Letter to the Ephesians (Eph 2: 19-22).

Indeed, according to an interpretation by Antonio Natali (1995) the five nudes holding draperies, leaning against the wall of an unfinished building could allude to the Gentiles engaged in stripping the old man to clothe the new man through baptism.

THE SISTINE CHAPEL – THE CEILING

"I hereby state that on this 10th day of May in the year fifteen hundred eight, I Michelangelo sculptor received from His Holiness, Pope Julius II, five hundred ducats […] for the painting of the ceiling of the chapel of Pope Sixtus on which I shall begin work today." And it was Michelangelo himself who tells us the date he began working on the chapel ceiling. The huge room, with dimensions similar to the Temple of Solomon, had been built about forty years earlier by Sixtus IV and was inaugurated with its just-finished frescoes on 15 August 1483, the Feast of the Assumption, and dedicated to the Assumption of the Virgin Mary.

Michelangelo accepted the commission for the titanic undertaking against his will, with his thoughts on much more stimulating work: the tomb that the same Pope Julius II had commissioned in 1505 but then changed his mind about and gave priority to other projects. Therefore, it was no accident that in 1508 the artist accepted the contract for the frescoes in the Sistine Chapel. He defiantly signed it as Michelangelo "sculptor" and frequently reiterated his "title" in letters written during that period.

Sistine Chapel,
Vatican City, Palazzi Vaticani.

The ceiling was partially unveiled when Michelangelo had finished the first half, on 15 August 1511, once again on the Feast of the Assumption. He completed it in October of the following year. The definitive inauguration took place on 1 November 1512, All Saints' Day. In a letter to his father he wrote: "I have finished the chapel I was painting: the pope was very satisfied."

Before Michelangelo put his hand to the chapel, the existing decorations were arranged in a regular wall-to-wall relationship that permitted a horizontal reading. On three walls we can still see the bands of the XV century fresco: at the top, next to the windows is the series of *Popes* by Domenico Ghirlandaio, Sandro Botticelli, Cosimo Rosselli and Fra' Diamante; in the center *Stories of Moses and Christ* (1481-1483) by the finest painters then working in Tuscany and Umbria: Perugino, Botticelli, Cosimo Rosselli, Luca Signorelli and Ghirlandaio with the assistance of others including Pinturicchio, Bartolomeo della Gatta, Piero di Cosimo (the two scenes on the wall facing the altar are late XVI century remakes). And finally, in the lower band, mock hangings which, during solemn ceremonies, were covered with real tapestries woven to cartoons by Raphael (1515-1516) and that is subsequent to Michelangelo's ceiling but prior to the *Last Judgment*. What we no longer see today, but was before Michelangelo's eyes in 1508, are the decorations on the wall behind the altar, the lunettes above the windows and the ceiling. On the altar wall there were two

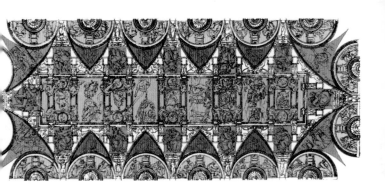

	Central Panels	- **Scenes from Genesis**
	Lateral Panels	- **The Seers (Prophets and Sibyls)**
	Triangles	- **Ancestors of Christ**
	Pendentives	- **Miraculous Salvation of Israel**
	Lunettes	- **Ancestors of Christ**

On pages 460-461,
ceiling of the Sistine Chapel, 1508-1512,
fresco, 1300 x 3600 cm;
Vatican City, Palazzi Vaticani, Sistine Chapel.

windows flanked by figures of popes, and there were three frescoes by Perugino: the first two stories of the cycles of the middle band and an altarpiece frescoed with the *Assumption of the Virgin* (which was entirely deleted to make room for the *Last Judgment* see pages 542-577); on the ceiling Piermatteo d'Amelia had painted a simple starry sky. The need to redecorate the ceiling arose from the damage caused to the existing frescoes when a huge crack appeared in the ceiling. And so the lapis lazuli ceiling was "covered" by one of the greatest masterpieces of all time.

Today, the fact that when the decision was made to re-paint the ceiling and the assignment was given to Michelangelo, cannot but be considered surprising since his fame at the time was certainly not related to painting. Indeed, he had done very little. Even Bramante, one of the great talents at the papal court, and close advisor to Julius II, repeatedly emphasized the fact and voiced his opposition stating "I believe that he [Michelangelo] hasn't sufficient spirit [for the task] because he has not done many figures." In spite of this the pope showed that he had unlimited faith in Buonarroti's ability and absolutely wanted to give him the commission. By so doing the pope, willingly or not, was launching a challenge between two supreme artists much like the one that had placed Michelangelo against his rival Leonardo in Palazzo della Signoria in Florence. Indeed, while Buonarroti was frescoing the ceiling in the chapel, the young Raphael was working on the decorations in the *Stanze Vaticane* to

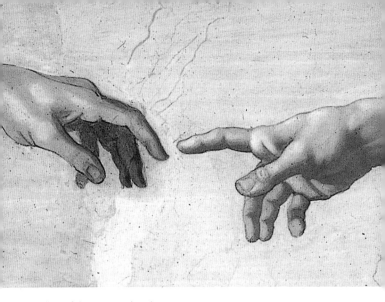

Ceiling of the Sistine Chapel,
Detail of *The Creation of Adam*.

On page 465, ceiling of the Sistine Chapel,
Ignudo on the left above the *Prophet Joel*.

On page 467, ceiling of the Sistine Chapel,
detail of *The Original Sin*.

On page 469, ceiling of the Sistine Chapel, detail of the *Bronze Ignudi*
and the triangle with *The future king Roboam* (*Ancestors of Christ*).

On page 471, ceiling of the Sistine Chapel,
Caryatid putti next to the *Prophet Daniel*.

On page 473, ceiling of the Sistine Chapel,
The Libyan Sybil.

the admiration of all. But this time things were different because Raphael considered Michelangelo a master, and the Tuscan genius seemed to respect the young man from Urbino. An amazed Raphael was present when the ceiling was partially unveiled by order of the pope in 1511 and he subsequently rendered homage to Buonarroti in his fresco of the *School of Athens* in the nearby papal apartment. He portrayed the artist as Heraclitus (see pages 68-69) and used the power of the Sistine frescoes as a model for other paintings in the *Stanze*.

The original iconographic program agreed upon for the chapel was quite simple. Michelangelo was to paint the twelve apostles in the lateral pendentives and triangles, and architectural decorations in the center. Instead, on this immense ceiling, of more than five hundred square meters, the master's incomparable brush told the story of humanity, from the primordial chaos to the promise of Salvation. It is a grandiose prologue to the advent of Christ animated by nearly three hundred thirty-six figures, a perfect group of plastic shapes and brilliant colors framed by painted architecture that seems to open outwards, liberated from the strict Renaissance rules of perspective.

In a letter from 1523 Michelangelo gave himself all the credit for the ambitious plan writing that since the original design seemed "so poor" to him, the pope gave "a new order that I could do what I want, what pleased me." However, given the complexity and the density of the al-

legorical and theological meanings expressed in the ceiling it is hard to believe that a similar cycle of frescoes could have been the fruit of one imagination alone, even if it was the imagination of the most brilliant artist. The more likely hypothesis is that Michelangelo collaborated with the learned theologians of the papal court who would have suggested themes and ideas that the artist then developed in his own style.

The names of these scholars have been suggested as the Franciscan, Marco Vigerio, and Egidio da Viterbo who had studied with Marsilio Ficino in Florence. And it is precisely a neo-Platonic reading of the ceiling that prevailed among critics even if a recent proposal suggests that Michelangelo's frescoes can be interpreted in relation to Savonarola's sermons.

Looking at the subjects, the central portion of the ceiling is decorated with nine – alternating five small and four large-panels with scenes from *Genesis.*

In the corners are pairs of male nudes, the famous *Ignudi,* in dynamic poses, holding bronze medallions with stories from the Books of Samuel and Kings. Following the logical-chronological of the nine central scenes, in the first six are scenes of the Creation: *The Division of Light from Darkness, The Creation of the Stars, The Separation of the Waters, The Creation of Adam, The Creation of Eve,* and the *Original Sin and Expulsion;* these are followed by three stories of Noah: *The Sacrifice of Noah, The Flood; The Drunkenness of Noah.* In the lateral panels around the central portion are the imposing – each with his or her

name on a plaque supported by a putto – seven *Prophets* and five *Sibyls*. Although from the pagan world, the group includes those who had heralded the advent of Christ (In the XII century the *Dies Irae* already read "Teste David cum Sibylla."). In the triangles and lunettes Michelangelo painted the *Ancestors of Christ* from Abraham to Joseph. In the lateral pendentives – surmounted by bronze nudes as are the vertices of the triangles – are four scenes from the Old Testament alluding to the messianic promise: *The Bronze Serpent, The Punishment of Haman, David and Goliath,* and *Judith and Holofernes.* The several parts are joined by painted architecture, while the heroic figures are subject to hierarchical and expressive proportions of an almost distant, archaic inspiration.

We could say that, in a way, Buonarroti was forced into his choices by the iconographic arrangement beneath the ceiling, that is the two, late XV century frescoed bands on the long walls of the chapel with the *Stories of Moses* and *Stories of Jesus*, and above these the series of *Popes*. Obviously, Michelangelo had little choice but to go farther back in time, starting from the beginning of the world. In any case, it is interesting to note that his earliest biographers say nothing about the allegorical interpretation of Michelangelo's masterpiece and limit themselves to pure and simple, though highly detailed, descriptions.

Tradition has it that the artist completed the frescoes entirely on his own, working in solitude without any

helpers. Actually, the restoration of the ceiling in the late nineteen eighties revealed that he did have a limited amount of help mainly on the first three stories in the central panels (Noah) and the secondary elements such as the *tondos*, reliefs, thrones and decorations.

However, everything was done under Michelangelo's close and direct control and he certainly did not leave his helpers the margin of freedom that they would normally have had working with other famous artists of the time (such as his own early teacher, Ghirlandaio).

He dedicated a great deal of time to the meticulously detailed preparatory cartoons for nearly all the figures (they have been lost). For the complex work of transposition, he called on some Florentine artists, including his friend Granacci whom he fired because he was not satisfied. Michelangelo worked on scaffolding attached to the walls, proceeding from the chapel entrance towards the altar, from *The Drunkenness of Noah* to *The Division of Light from Darkness*, and worked on the architectural bands perpendicular to the long walls as if they were the intradoses of triumphal arches. For the first half of the ceiling the cartoons were transposed by pouncing – except for a few figures; in the second half, even though pouncing was used on some parts, on the main scenes he almost always used a stylus to trace the designs incising them onto the surface, a method that calls for faster and more "spontaneous" fresco painting. The exception is the *Creation of Adam*, where signs of both techniques are evident.

The sequence of the painting of the central biblical scenes corresponds to the order of reading proposed by the artist, that is, going back in time from the *Stories of Noah* to the first day of *Creation*. By following this chronological and visual path we can see how the artist's style matured, to the point of achieving greater structural monumentality and increased luminosity in the scenes and figures of the second part.

The recent restorations of the ceiling also brought to light the original colors that had been darkened by centuries of dirt and soot: light, cold, transparent colors; unnatural colors (totally different, for example, from those used by Michelangelo's Venetian contemporaries) colors "of the soul" already experimented in the *Doni Tondo* and forerunners of the Mannerist palette.

Ceiling of the Sistine Chapel,
The Division of Light from Darkness.

Ceiling of the Sistine Chapel,
Ignudo on the left above
the *Prophet Jeremiah*.

Ceiling of the Sistine Chapel,
Ignudo on the right above
the *Prophet Jeremiah*.

Ceiling of the Sistine Chapel,
The Creation of the Stars.

Ceiling of the Sistine Chapel, *The Separation of the Waters*.

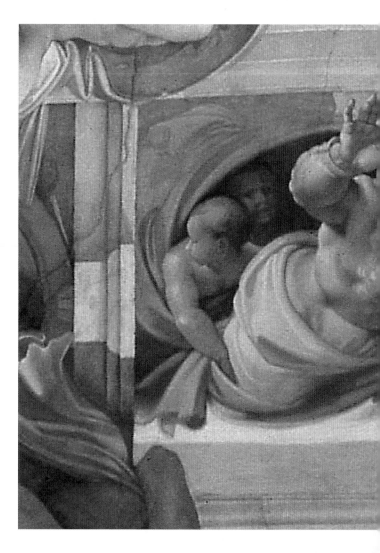

Ceiling of the Sistine Chapel,
The Creation of Adam.

Ceiling of the Sistine Chapel, *The Creation of Eve*.

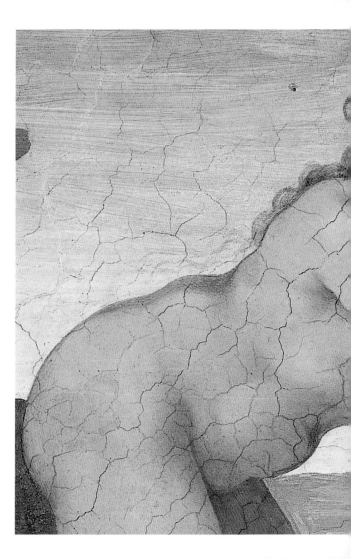

Ceiling of the Sistine Chapel,
The Original Sin and Expulsion.

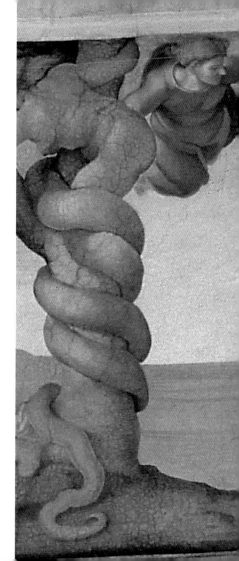

Ceiling of the Sistine Chapel,
The Sacrifice of Noah.

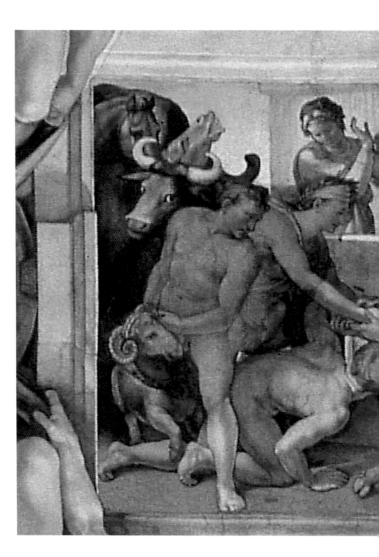

Ceiling of the Sistine Chapel,
The Flood.

Ceiling of the Sistine Chapel,
The Drunkenness of Noah.

Ceiling of the Sistine
Chapel,
The Bronze Serpent.

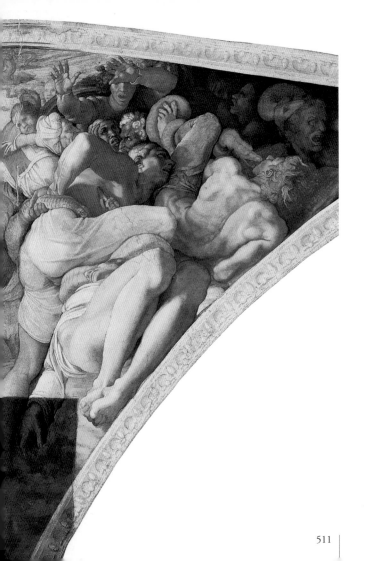

Ceiling of the Sistine
Chapel: left,
The Libyan Sybil;
lunette,
The future king Jesse.

Ceiling of the Sistine
Chapel: left,
The Prophet Daniel;
lunette,
The future king Asa.

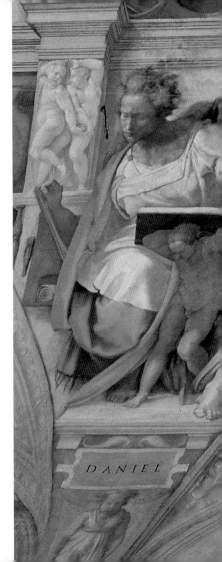

DANIEL

ASA
IOSAPHAT
IORAM

Ceiling of the Sistine
Chapel: left,
The Cumean Sybil;
lunette,
The future king Ezechia.

CVMAEA

Ceiling of the Sistine
Chapel: left,
The Prophet Isaiah;
lunette,
*The future king Josiah
with his father and mother.*

Ceiling of the Sistine
Chapel,
The Delphic Sybil.

Ceiling of the Sistine
Chapel,
Judith and Holofernes.

Ceiling of the Sistine
Chapel,
The Prophet Zechariah.

526

Ceiling of the Sistine
Chapel,
David and Goliath.

Ceiling of the Sistine
Chapel: left,
The Prophet Joel;
lunette,
*The future king
Zorobabel*.

ERITHRAEA

Ceiling of the Sistine
Chapel: left,
The Erythrean Sybil;
lunette,
The future king Ozias.

EZECHIEL

Ceiling of the Sistine
Chapel: left,
The Prophet Ezekiel;
lunette,
The future king Roboam.

PERSICHA

Ceiling of the Sistine
Chapel: left,
The Persian Sibyl;
lunette,
The future king Solomon.

Ceiling of the Sistine
Chapel,
The Prophet Jeremiah.

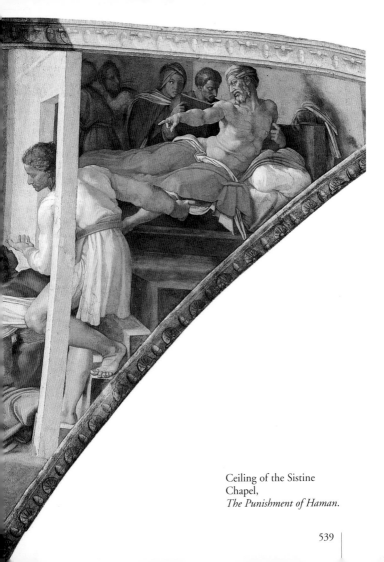

Ceiling of the Sistine
Chapel,
The Punishment of Haman.

Ceiling of the Sistine
Chapel,
The Prophet Jonah.

THE LAST JUDGMENT

Shortly after he became Pope Paul III, Alessandro Farnese, gave Michelangelo a task that had already been planned by his predecessor, Clement VII: to complete the decoration of the Sistine Chapel, with a grandiose *Last Judgment* on the wall behind the altar. In 1535 Michelangelo had the scaffolding built and prepared the wall by having it covered with bricks, of decreasing thickness to make the it slant slightly and thus facilitate vision from below. The following year, after twenty-four years, the artist was once again painting in the Sistine Chapel. The *Last Judgment* was completed in 1541 and unveiled on 31 October of that same year, for Vespers on the eve of All Saints' Day.

Last Judgment,
1535-1541,
fresco, 1370 x 1220 cm;
Vatican City, Palazzi Vaticani, Sistine Chapel.

543

The painting of the new fresco entailed the destruction of three works by Perugino and others, as well as two of the lunettes Michelangelo himself had done in 1512 as part of the ceiling decoration.

The enormous composition of the *Last Judgment* consists essentially of three bands crowned by the two lunettes. Nearly four hundred figures move in an abstract spatial arrangement without coordinates. Their sizes range from 250 cm at the top to 150 cm at the bottom. Wingless angels in the lunettes hold four symbols of the Passion: the Cross, the Crown, the Column and the Reed. In the uppermost band is the heavenly world. The center is dominated by the majestic Christ the Judge, portrayed as the "new Adam" without beard or the traditional throne. With his right hand raised and directed gaze He is poised to push the damned to hell, while the other hand is extended to summon the elect. They are watched by the comforting, serene gaze of Mary who confirms the salvation desired by the Son. In a circle around Christ and the Virgin are saints, patriarchs and apostles, without haloes. They, in turn, are surrounded by martyrs, confessors of the Church, virgins and the blessed arranged in two lateral groups, forming a semicircle broken in the middle. Saints Lawrence and Bartholomew are prominently portrayed at Christ's feet, perhaps because the chapel was dedicated to them as well as the to Assumption. In the central band is the group of angels with the trumpets of the Last Judgment and the books of the sentences; on the

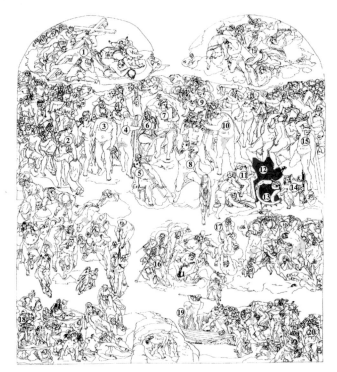

1. Archangel Gabriel (?)
2. Niobe (or Eve or the Church) (?)
3. Saint John the Baptist (or Adam)
4. Saint Andrew
5. Saint Lawrence
6. The Virgin Mary
7. Christ the Judge
8. Saint Bartholomew
9. Saint John the Evangelist (?)
10. Saint Peter (or Pope Paul III)
11. Dismas

12. Saint Blaise
13. Saint Catherine of Alexandria
14. Saint Sebastian
15. Simon the Cyrene
16. The Archangel Michael holding the Book of the Elect
17. The proud or the damned
18. Pope Clement VII (?)
19. Charon
20. Minos (Biagio da Cesena)

left are the redeemed, with adoring or incredulous expressions going up to the Kingdom of Heaven, while on the right the damned are tumbling into hell, rejected by the angels and dragged down by demons. And finally in the lowest band are: on the left the resurrection of the dead after the end of days and on the right the Hell, with Charon ferrying the souls of the damned to Minos for judgment. The cavern in the center has been interpreted as the mouth of Hell.

Michelangelo illustrated the theme of the *Last Judgment* with an anthology of magnificent scenes and unforgettable figures which, in part, were inspired by Dante Alighieri's *Divine Comedy*. His interest in that source is demonstrated by some of the sonnets he wrote and dedicated to the great poet in 1545-1546 after having completed the fresco; he planned on including them in the publication of his *Rime*.

Critics are unanimous in considering Michelangelo's *Last Judgment* a total innovation with respect to the traditional Italian iconography of the period. Not only are the figures arranged differently (especially the angels with the instruments of martyrdom and with the trumpets), but the composition is not divided into clearly distinct bands. It conveys the impression of a whirlpool created

Last Judgment,
detail, Christ the Judge.

by Christ's raised arm: a vortex of cyclopean figures suspended in bunches and not framed in any precise compositional schema.

Actually, recent studies have shown that the typology of Michelangelo's *Last Judgment* fits into the Nordic tradition of the subject that was handed down in Buffalmacco's XIV century fresco in the Camposanto in Pisa, which Buonarroti obviously knew, and confirmed for example by Rogier van der Weyden's painting in Beaune (1443-1451)

Michelangelo began working on the fresco from the top, specifically the lunette on the left and proceeded towards the bottom. He made preparatory cartoons for all the main figures: on the upper part the drawings were transferred by pouncing, the technique most suitable for a more finished fresco; in the lower portion he used the stylus tracing which creates a more sketched, less elaborate effect.

Prior to the 1990-1994 restorations, the surface of the fresco was very dirty. By bringing out the light, luminous colors the restoration has allowed critics and scholars to review their interpretation of the *Last Judgment* as an obscure, mysterious masterpiece in which *terribilità* of the subject seemed to be expressed in the dark colors. The tones which, over the years, had become dark and dull did not fail to inspire many XIX century romantic

Last Judgment,
detail, Saint Lawrence.

painters such as Blake and Delacroix who in *Dante's Boat* (1822) used dark colors just like those in the *Last Judgment* the way it looked then. Many, even violent, protests were directed against the cleaned, bright colors by scholars still tied to the idea of the "dirty" fresco, the way it had been known for centuries.

One of the most prominent pigments in the composition is the expensive lapis lazuli (ultramarine blue) that he used for creating the blues, and the intense color of the sky which is a determining factor in the overall effect. The cleaning also revealed a good number of – sometimes significant – corrections, additions and dry-finishing touches even done several *giornate,* that is working days, later.

In order to complete his grandiose undertaking, Michelangelo, who was usually reluctant to having helpers, did – especially at the beginning – work with his pupil Francesco Amadori, known as the Urbino. He probably worked on some of the figures of the resurrected when Michelangelo injured his leg in a fall from the scaffolding and the difference in quality is quite evident.

Tradition maintains that Michelangelo portrayed some of his contemporaries in the fresco: Saint Peter would resemble Paul III; Minos with the serpent entwined

Last Judgment,
detail, Saint Bartholomew.
The saint's flayed skin is believed
to be a self-portrait of Michelangelo.

around his body biting his testicles could be Biagio da Cesena the master of ceremonies who had criticized the fresco; Saint Bartholomew has been recognized as the writer Pietro Aretino, while on the martyr's skin in the saint's hand, would be a self-portrait of Michelangelo.

In 1545, four years after the unveiling of the *Last Judgment,* Paul III convened the Council of Trent. The Council was the Church's reaction to the advance of the Protestant Reformation, triggered by Martin Luther's Ninety Five Theses in 1517, as it spread through Northern Europe. Following the votes of the Council a wave of severity swept through the countries that remained loyal to the Church, with a series of measures based on the strictest observance of dogma. Among one of the Council's decisions – concluded in 1563, was the censuring of the nudes in the *Last Judgment* that were considered obscene. The decision was made in January 1564 one month before Michelangelo died on 18 February.

Last Judgment,
detail of the proud or damned.

The task of covering the scandalous nudity of the figures was given to his friend and pupil, Daniele Ricciarelli da Volterra. The *Braghettone* – drawers maker – as he was called because of the *braghe* (drawers) he painted onto the master's nudes, did the work in 1565. He usually used the *secco* or dry technique, except for a few cases such as Saint Blaise and Saint Catherine who were entirely nude and crouching one on top of the other in what was considered an ambiguous position. Daniele destroyed Michelangelo's painted plaster then he frescoed the green robe on Catherine and turned Saint Blaise in the other direction.

However, Daniele's cover-ups were not the only ones, in fact they continued to the end of the century and probably extended into the 1700s. As to the "drawers" the recent restoration was quite conservative and left Daniele da Volterra's and most of the other additions *in situ*, in keeping with the principle of leaving everything that has historical value.

Last Judgment,
detail, Minos.

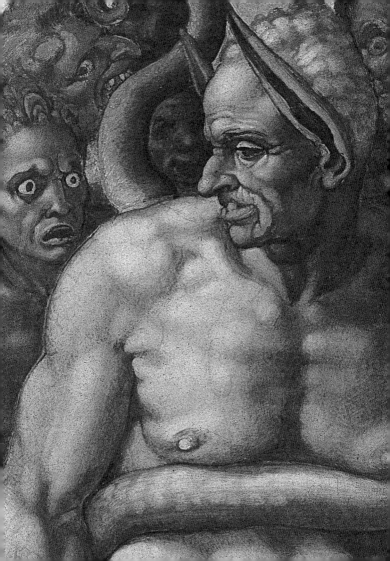

S

On pages 556-557,
Last Judgment,
detail of the left lunette,
with angels holding
the symbols of the Passion:
the cross and the crown of thorns.

On pages 558-559,
Last Judgment,
detail of the right lunette
with angels holding
the symbols of the Passion:
the column and the reed.

Left,
Last Judgment,
detail, the Elect to the left
of Christ the Judge: the figure
in the center with the fur
loincloth is Saint John
the Baptist; near him,
Saint Andrew with his X-shaped
cross is seen from the back.

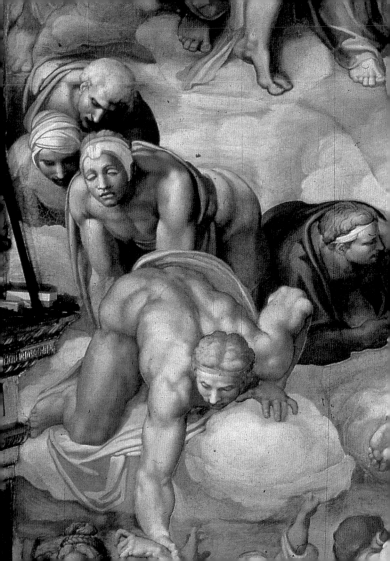

On page 562,
Last Judgment,
detail, center band, left:
the Redeemed helped by
angels rise to join the Blessed.

On page 563,
Last Judgment,
detail, the Elect to the right
of Christ the Judge.

Right,
Last Judgment,
detail, the Elect to the right
of Christ the Judge:
the powerful Saint Peter
holding the keys; the man
on the right holding the cross
is Dismas, the good thief,
or perhaps the Cyrene
who helped Christ
on the way to Calvary;
below the Apostle Simon
with the saw, the Apostle
Philip with the cross, Saint
Blaise with the iron combs,
Saint Catherine of Alessandria
with the wheel and Saint
Sebastian with the arrows.

Left,
Last Judgment, detail,
center band, left:
the elect helped by angels
rise to join the Blessed.

On pages 568-569,
Last Judgment,
Detail of the central part
of the center band:
angels with the trumpets
of the Last Judgment;
in the foreground the books
of judgement – the "book
of life" which is smaller
is open towards the elect,
the other with the sentences
is open towards the damned
and Charon.

Right,
Last Judgment,
detail, center band, right:
the damned being banished
to hell by the angels.

On pages 572-573 and 574,
Last Judgment,
detail, lower band, left:
the resurrection of the bodies.

On page 575,
Last Judgment, detail,
lower band, right:
the damned
on Charon's boat.

On pages 576-577,
Last Judgment, detail,
lower band, right:
the damned arriving
in Hell; left, Charon;
right, Minos.

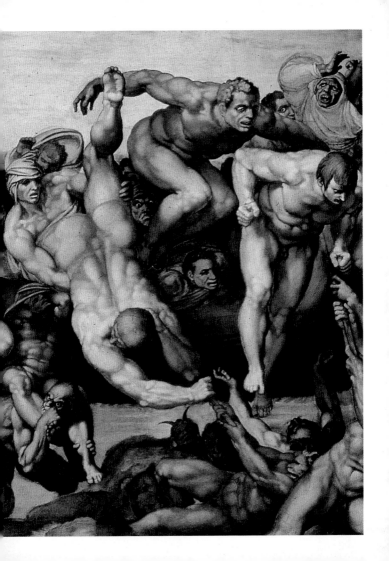

STORIES OF SAINTS PETER AND PAUL IN THE PAULINE CHAPEL

Michelangelo had barely completed the *Last Judgment* in the Sistine Chapel when, in 1541, Paul III commissioned him to fresco the walls of the Pauline Chapel, the pope's private chapel built by Antonio da Sangallo and inaugurated the previous year. Michelangelo, who was already seventy, began the work in 1542 and continued it, with several interruptions due to failing health and a fire that broke out in 1545. Completed in 1550, the two frescoes depict culminating episodes from the lives of the two main apostles: the *Conversion of Saul* who became Saint Paul – the name Alessandro Farnese took when elected pope – and the *Crucifixion of St Peter*. At first he had planned on associating the scene of the conversion with the delivery of the keys to Saint Peter. The final iconographic choice aims at highlighting "two essential moments of the religious life or human existence, conversion and martyrdom" (Argan 1963).

In the *Conversion of Saul,* the apostle – considered to be a self portrait of the aging artist – is thrown to the ground and blinded by the light of Jesus shining from above. Jesus performs a dual gesture, with one hand he points to Damascus in the distance where Saul had been going to persecute Christians, while with the other, open and extended he projects the light to the ground. The luminous horizon divides the scene into two groups, driven by

Conversion of Saul,
1542-1545,
fresco, 625 x 661 cm;
Vatican City, Palazzi Vaticani,
Pauline Chapel.

centripetal and centrifugal forces, respectively. In the upper part the angels move towards Christ in a circle, below the disconcerted soldiers flee in different directions. Saul, on the ground, raises his torso towards the light from which he is also defending himself. His pose repeats the solution of the model of the *River God* for the New Sacristy (see pages 304-307).

The *Crucifixion of St Peter* portrays the moment in which the cross is about to be driven into the ground. The onlookers isolate the group in the middle, encircling the diagonally placed cross and the executioners who are raising it. One the left they are going up the ridge and on the right descending; they dialogue silently, with solemn, subdued gestures expressing despair and resignation The fulcrum of the composition is Peter's head that is raised in contrast with the motion of the cross and he looks at the viewer while his body slides on the wood.
Both scenes are constructed against a rugged, essential and abstract landscape in which the solitary, heroic figures, absolute protagonists of their story stand out.

Crucifixion of Saint Peter,
1546-1550,
fresco, 625 x 662 cm;
Vatican City, Palazzi Vaticani,
Pauline Chapel.

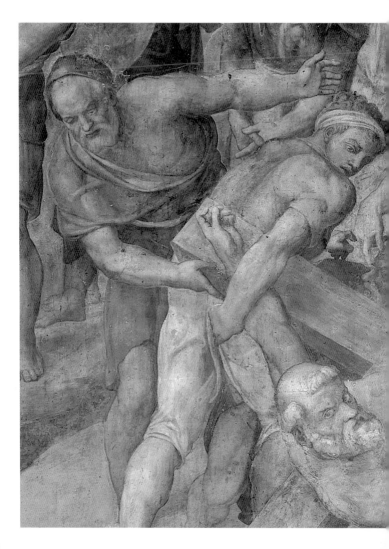

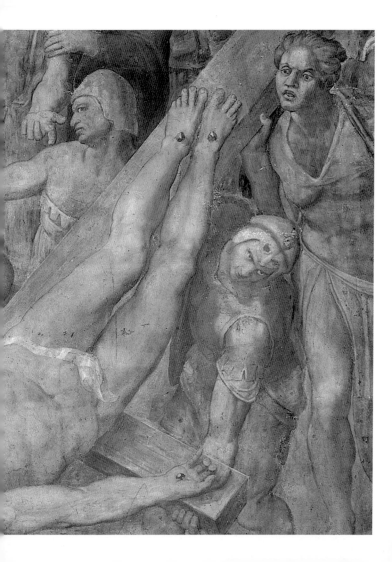

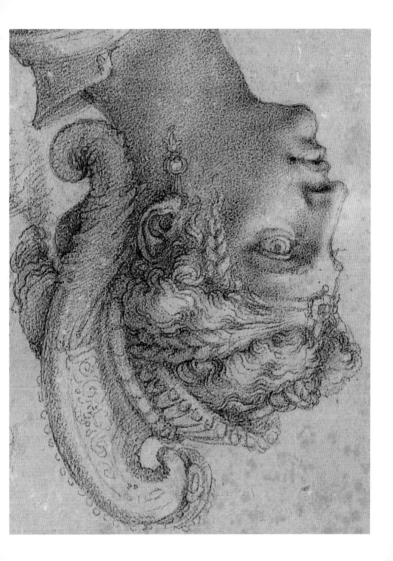

Drawings

"Painting, sculpture and architecture culminate in drawing. This is the primary source and soul of all manners of painting and the roots of all science," with this statement recorded in Francisco de Hollanda's *Dialogues* Michelangelo theorized the primacy of drawing over any form of artistic expression. It is in the drawing that the idea, conceived in the artist's mind, takes form before it becomes reality. Vasari (1568) tells us that Michelangelo destroyed many sheets, but in spite of this, the *corpus* of his surviving drawings is still enormous. There are copies of traditional Florentine and ancient models, many preparatory studies for sculptures, paintings and architecture, "presentation drawings" completed compositions and the splendid ideal heads – often female – that Vasari called "divine heads" which are a particularly fascinating aspect of Michelangelo's drawings. In his later years he gave some drawings, to two very close friends: Tommaso de' Cavalieri, the handsome, educated Roman gentlemen whom he frequented in 1531-1532 and Vittoria Colonna, Marchesa of Pescara whom he first met in 1536. As Vasari writes, Michelangelo made "many drawings for friends," inventions on paper that others would have probably transposed into paintings.

Zenobia or Ideal Head,
detail, 1525;
Florence, Gabinetto Disegni
e Stampe degli Uffizi, inv. 598 Er.

DAMNED SOUL OR FURY

The three drawings Gherardo Perini received from Michelangelo were bequeathed to the collection of Francesco I, grand duke of Florence upon his death. This was destined to become the most famous and most widely copied of Michelangelo's drawings. Not done for any specific project, but as a gift of friendship it portrays the face of a mature man with his mouth open in a furious scream, with a correspondingly violent expression in his eyes. The wind-blown hair emphasizes a leftward motion, while the gaze is directed to the right. A full cloak, raised by the wind frames the face. It is probably an allegorical image and could have been inspired by a piece by Leonardo da Vinci listed as *Infernal Fury* in a XVI century inventory. The recipient's name, Gherardo Perini is at the top, while Michelangelo's symbol of three interlocking circles is in the bottom right corner: the symbol alludes to the three main arts, painting, sculpture and architecture. Michelangelo used a very soft black charcoal and created a very full, plastic effect by allowing the paper to show through. Unfortunately, the drawing is not well conserved.

Damned Soul or Fury,
1525, black chalk, 298 x 205 mm;
Florence, Gabinetto Disegni
e Stampe degli Uffizi, inv. 601 E.

ZENOBIA OR IDEAL HEAD

According to Vasari in the first edition of *Lives* (1550), Michelangelo himself said, this drawing was done "out of love not obligation," for Gherardo Perini. The writer tells us that Perini received a gift of three drawings of heads. There are no stories or scenes, just "divine heads" characterized by unusual expressions. The one known as Zenobia is a special subject. Early inventories do not list or define the details. In 1560 it is described as a female head with an ancient headdress, then as a *Zingbana*, or gypsy, from which the title probably developed over the years. Zenobia was a resolute warrior queen of Palmyra in the III century who was defeated by Aurelian. The image of the young woman is Eastern, with her bosom high above a corselet; on her head she wears an ancient-style diadem that holds back her hair.

On the same sheet there are also the heads of a child and an old man in a subordinate position. The child would be her son, the man her husband whom, according to Boccaccio, Zenobia only wed in order to have children. The drawings Michelangelo gave Perini are not in good condition, but this is the best conserved and most complete.

Zenobia or Ideal Head,
1525, charcoal, 375 x 252 mm;
Florence, Gabinetto Disegni
e Stampe degli Uffizi, inv. 598 Er.

The Archers

This red chalk drawing is probably one of the "presentation drawings" Michelangelo did for a friend. Although it is not included in Vasari's list of drawings for Tommaso de' Cavalieri, it may have been a gift for his dear Roman friend. The group in the center consists of two women, seven men and two *putti* all facing right and seized in the moment of shooting an arrow although only one of them has a bow. At the far right of the sheet, that was cut on all four sides, there is a shield held by a herm already pierced by some arrows. At the herm's feet is a sleeping Cupid with a quiver by his side. On the other side two *putti*, ignoring the archers and almost knocked over by them, are feeding a fire with two bunches of wood. The archery contest seems to be taking place between humans and divinities, and we can recognize Diana, the powerful figure on the left.

The source is a probably a stucco from Nero's *Domus Aurea*. The allegorical meaning, however, is more hidden and has often been interpreted as a portrayal of how rarely love's arrows hit their targets. The *putti* on the left, therefore, symbolize the difficulties they encounter on the way. The scene could also be a materialization of Cupid's dream or represent his resignation in seeing his followers' lack of skill.

The Archers,
1530-1533, red chalk, 219 x 323 mm:
Windsor, Royal Library, inv. 12778.

Rape of Ganymede

This drawing belongs to the series Michelangelo made for his friend Tommaso de' Cavalieri. The first information about this drawing is in a letter Tommaso wrote to Michelangelo on 6 September 1533, telling him how much both Pope Clement VII and Cardinal Ippolito de' Medici admired his drawing. In fact, the cardinal had requested a crystal copy of *Ganymede* and the *Punishment of Tityus*. It is probably no coincidence that the two drawings are mentioned together. They were, in fact, made as a sort of diptych with a young male nude and a bird as the subjects of both. The handsome Ganymede, shepherd son of the king of Troy was taken to Olympus because Jupiter fell in love with him. According to Ovid (*Metamorphoses*) the god transformed himself into an eagle, and took the youth to Olympus to make him his cup-bearer.

There are two known versions of this drawing, one is at the Uffizi in Florence and the other Cambridge, Massachusetts. In the latter the youth is portrayed with a blissful expression while he lets himself be seized by his lover. At the bottom of the sheet is a sketch of dog barking upwards, and next to him the youth's abandoned hunting implements. The subject Michelangelo selected for this gift reveals the feelings the artist had for the young Tommaso de' Cavalieri.

Rape of Ganymede,
1532-1533, charcoal, 380 x 270 mm;
Cambridge, Fogg Art Museum, inv. 1955.75.

THE PUNISHMENT OF TITYUS

Ovid tells the story of Tityus in the *Metamorphoses*. Tityus was a giant who tried to kidnap the mother of Apollo and Diana, but was killed by their arrows. First he was tortured: his hands and feet were tied to the ground and his liver was devoured by vultures.

In antiquity the liver was considered the seat of all emotions. Artists usually portray the scene with one bird, and Michelangelo did likewise. He portrays the youth with one wrist tied to a rock and turned downwards; above him there is an eagle aiming at the bare chest with his beak but not wounding him. Michelangelo added variations and does not portray the actual torture which would have been an allegory of the body's enslavement to sensual pleasures. Instead, the reference to the Ganymede drawing, the other half of the pair, is quite explicit. The eagle is the same, and the youth also has blond curls. The drawing, therefore, alludes to the agonies caused by amorous passion, and was yet another gift to Michelangelo's friend Tommaso de' Cavalieri.

His use of chalk for the trunk and rock makes the figures very different from the surrounding landscape and seems to have been a deliberate choice on the part of the artist.

The Punishment of Tityus,
1532, black chalk, 190 x 330 mm:
Windsor Castle, Royal Library, inv. 12771.

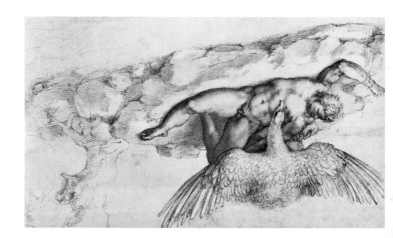

THE FALL OF PHAETON

There are three extant versions of this drawing by Michelangelo, and the most famous is in the Windsor Castle collection. And that is the one Michelangelo made for his friend Tommaso de' Cavalieri. The artist portrays the drama of Apollo's son who is punished by Jupiter because he tried to drive the chariot of the Sun. As we read in Ovid's *Metamorphoses*, Buonarroti depicts Jupiter at the top, astride an eagle and about to throw a bolt of lightning at Phaeton. The youth is backwards as he falls into the River Eridanus, together with his horses; the river is symbolized by an old man with a flowing beard on the ground next to a vase pouring water. The three female figures are Phaeton's sisters, the Heliads who were transformed into poplar trees out of grief, and next to them is Cygnus the youth's friend who was changed into a swan. The drawing is very dramatic and is characterized by great formal care. The twisting figures are highlighted with great strength.

The drawing was an immediate success and was copied many times to become a favorite among engravers. Michelangelo's initial inspiration came from his study of a Roman sarcophagus that is now in the Uffizi.

The Fall of Phaeton,
1533, charcoal, 413 x 234 mm;
Windsor Castle, Royal Library, inv. 12766.

BACCHANAL OF CHILDREN

This is probably the last drawing Michelangelo made for Tommaso de' Cavalieri. The "presentation drawings" portray complex subjects and are inspired by mythological tales and ancient works of art. In this case, however, the scene seems to be the artist's own invention. There are five groups of lively children in an "X" formation in a grotto. The center group is struggling with the body of an animal; other children are grouped around a fire with a cauldron. On the side, some are gathered around a vat, some are diving into it, others are drinking the wine.

In the lower portion of the drawing, a virile male nude is being covered by a child; in another corner there is a "satyresque" old woman with sagging breasts who is nursing a child while another sleeps on her lap. The theme may be an allegory of the soul dulled and darkened by vice, but in any case, it is difficult to understand the meaning. Michelangelo did the drawing while in Florence, sad and depressed because his friend Tommaso was far away.

The classical references are evident, along with citations of Donatello's art. From the technical standpoint, Michelangelo used the potential of the white paper to the fullest, leaving it visible in the more luminous areas to create a strong plastic effect.

Bacchanal of Children,
1533, red chalk, 274 x 388 mm;
Windsor Castle, Royal Library, inv. 12777.

CLEOPATRA

Michelangelo did this drawing for Tommaso dé' Cavalieri, the young nobleman he met in 1532. It is one of the many "presentation drawings," that is gifts rather than studies, that he made for friends. The subjects are all very complex and always secular in nature.

In 1562 Tommaso was forced to sell the drawing and that is how it came into the hands of Cosimo I, Grand Duke of Florence. She is portrayed with bare shoulders and breast; her head is turned to the left so it is almost a full-face rendering revealing a long, sensual neck. Her hair is held in place by bands and a long braid winds around the chignon and comes down on her left shoulder; the serpent wound around her neck biting her breast seems to come from her hair. The iconography has a precedent: the painting known as *Simonetta Vespucci*, by the Florentine artist Piero di Cosimo (Chantilly, Musée Condé). A 1988 restoration revealed another, autograph drawing on the other side of the sheet. The paper had been lined, perhaps by Michelangelo himself. The other drawing, which is undefined and incomplete, also portrays the queen of Egypt, but with a pained and anguished expression; there is also a barely sketched profile of an old man with a prominent nose and chin that recalls Leonardo da Vinci's drawings.

Cleopatra,
1533-1534, black chalk, 232 x 182 mm;
Florence, Casa Buonarroti, inv. 2 F.

CHRIST ON THE CROSS
(WITH GRIEVING ANGELS)

This drawing was made as a gift for Vittoria Colonna. After ten years Michelangelo was once again make "pre-sentation drawings" for friends. The drawings for the marchesa had different origins: Condivi relates that she had asked to watch the artist at work so that she could request modifications as indeed seems to have happened. This different approach had its roots in the exchange of ideas that bound the two – either poems or religious subjects within the context of the interiorization of the faith that guided the Roman religious *milieu*.

Christ is portrayed with the most skillful use of the medium; tiny chalk strokes create a particularly luminous effect, leaving the grain of the white paper clearly visible. The Christ seems alive, and suffering, with mouth open appealing to the Father; next to Him are the angels and Adam's skull – the symbol of Original Sin cancelled by Jesus' sacrifice – is at the foot of the cross. The marchesa had a profound understanding of all these elements. Her appreciation of the drawing was spiritual as well as esthetic as we can see from her own words: "… I certainly recall other Crucifixions, but never have I seen an image so finely drawn, so alive and so completely finished."

Christ on the Cross with Grieving Angels,
c. 1540, black chalk, 370 x 270 mm;
London, British Museum,
Department of Prints and Drawings, inv. 1895-9-15-504.

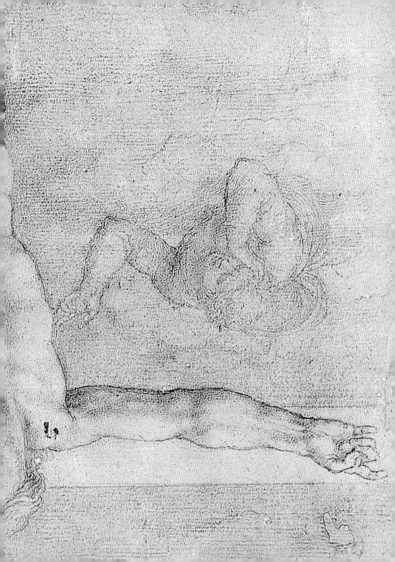

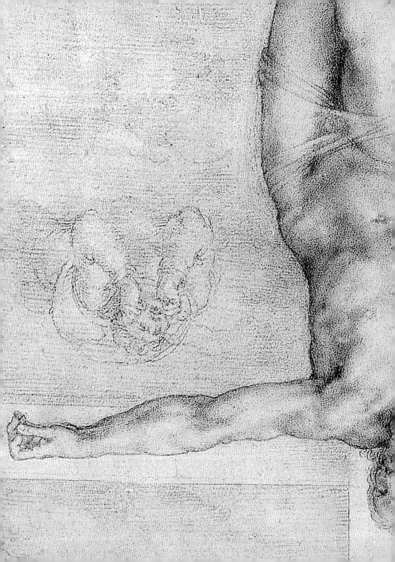

PIETÀ FOR VITTORIA COLONNA

Condivi (1553) is the first source who mentions the drawings Michelangelo did for Vittoria Colonna: the *Crucifix*, the *Pietà* and the *Good Samaritan*. He tells us that it was Vittoria Colonna who suggested the subject and composition for this drawing of the *Pietà*. Mary is portrayed as the intermediary between the sins of mankind and heaven. It is a drawing focused on the religious teachings dear to the group of church reformers the marchesa herself belonged to. The cross is triangular, like the processional cross used by the Compagnia dei Bianchi of Florence, and it has an inscription from Canto XXIX of *Paradise*, by Dante Alighieri, "Men think not how much blood it costs." It is a very austere composition: at the foot of the cross, Christ's lifeless body is held by two small angels. The Virgin Mary is portrayed with eyes and arms raised up to heaven, almost as if to balance the body of Christ that is heavily sliding downward. In this way the bodies form another cross. The drama of the scene is revealed by the Virgin's grieving face – and yet she accepts destiny with faith. These drawings were objects of devotion for the marchesa and strengthened her affectionate ties with the master.

Pietà for Vittoria Colonna, or *Mater Dolorosa*,
c. 1541, charcoal, 295 x 195 mm;
Boston, Isabella Stewart Gardner Museum, inv. 1.2.o/16.0.

ANNUNCIATION

Leonardo Buonarroti, the artist's nephew and heir, gave this drawing to the Grand Duke Cosimo I after Michelangelo died. Vasari tells us that towards the end of his life Michelangelo had burned many of his drawings that the grand duke had not considered worthy of the genius. Actually, Cosimo I was very sorry because he had thus lost an artistic treasure to which he believed he had rights. As early as 1561 he had already a compiled an album of drawings by the greatest artists. Vasari himself advised Leonardo Buonarroti to present the drawings that were still in the Via Mozza studio in Florence to make up for his uncle's "mistake." Leonardo added other drawings, including this one. Michelangelo had made it for the sculptor Jacopo del Duca, one of his last pupils, but it had to be returned, to enhance the gift to the grand duke. Originally the attribution to Michelangelo was doubtful because of a painting by Marcello Venusti based on the drawing (church of San Giovanni in Laterano in Rome). Today it has been confirmed as Michelangelo's; it was probably one of the drawings for friends that he sent to be colored by others. Venusti was one of those artists and then used the subject for his own painting.

Annunciation,
c. 1550, black chalk, 405 x 545 mm;
Florence, Gabinetto Disegni
e Stampe degli Uffizi, inv. 229 F.

Self-portrait of the artist painting the Sistine Ceiling,
with the sonnet *Io ho già fatto un gozzo in questo stento*, 1509-1510,
pen and ink, 283 x 200 mm;
Florence, Casa Buonarroti, Archivio Buonarroti, inv. XIII/111.

Poetry

Michelangelo wrote poetry – sonnets, canzone, madrigals and capitoli – short burlesque poems in *terza rima*. He wrote on and off and never had any definite thoughts about publishing his poems. There were periods of fervent writing – the years of his friendship with Tommaso de' Cavalieri, whom he met in 1532 and Vittoria Colonna, she too a poet whom he frequented until she died in 1547. During his lifetime manuscripts with his poems began circulating within a small circle of literati, including Francesco Berni, Benedetto Varchi, Donato Giannotti and Luigi del Riccio. Berni, who dubbed the artist "Apollo-Apelles," and recognized the original expressive power and conceptual profundity of Michelangelo's poems with respect to the then fashionable – and superficial – Petrarchism "he says things says you say words..." Luigi Del Riccio wanted to publish a selection of the poems, but he died in 1546 before he could do so. Since then, Michelangelo's poetry remained more or less in oblivion. In 1623 Michelangelo Buonarroti the Younger published the first edition of his famous ancestor's poems, but he modified and cut them. Only in the XIX century did a new, enlarged version appear, edited by Cesare Guasti (1863) and based on the autograph poems; and this was followed, a hundred years later, by the Enzo Noè Girari (1960) and Matteo Residori (1998) editions.

SONNET WITH A SELF-PORTRAIT OF THE ARTIST PAINTING THE SISTINE CEILING

Michelangelo wrote this poem as a young man in Rome while frescoing the ceiling of the Sistine Chapel for Pope Julius II. In fact, the autograph version includes a sketch of himself standing with his head tilted back while painting the *Creation of the sun and the moon*, which means the period that he was working on the second part of the decorations. This is an interesting document because it sheds light on his painting position, often believed to have been stretched out on the boards. Beneath his feet are a few lines that form a ladder, probably part of the scaffolding. The tone of the sonnet is witty and ironic: he describes himself with ridiculous similes, complaining about his task. His body, suspended in the air is twisted and tense, like a "Syrian bow", the type Michelangelo was familiar with because Lorenzo the Magnificent had one as per the 1492 inventory. This bow must have been so curved that the grip protruded, like the artist's belly judging from his caricature. The original includes a dedication to Giovanni da Pistoia, academician and humanist whom Michelange-lo is reminding that he is not a painter, almost as if to beg pardon for his work and complaints. The fine, elongated script is typical of Buonarroti's early years.

I've grown a goiter by dwelling in this den
Like cats from stagnant streams in Lombardy,
Or in what other land they happen to be
Which drives the belly close beneath the chin:
My beard turns up to heaven; my nape falls in,
Fixed on my spine: my breast-bone visibly
Grows like a harp: a rich embroidery
Bedews my face from brush-drops thick and thin.
My loins into my paunch like levers grind:
My buttock like a crupper bears my weight;
My feet unguided wander to and fro;
In front my skin grows loose and long; behind,
By bending it becomes more taut and strait;
Crosswise I strain me like a Syrian bow:
Whence false and quaint, I know,
Must be the fruit of squinting brain and eye;
For ill can one aim the gun that bends awry.
Come then, Giovanni, try
To succor my dead pictures and my fame;
Since foul I fare and painting is my shame

Io ho già fatto un gozzo in questo stento,
sonnet, 1509-1510;
Florence, Casa Buonarroti, Archivio Buonarroti, inv. XIII/111.

SONNET ON THE "CONCEPT" OF SCULPTING MARBLE

This is both one of Michelangelo's most famous sonnets and one of the most important for an understanding of the Neoplatonic artistic theory. It was highly praised by his contemporaries, including Benedetto Varchi who used it as the main subject of his first *Lezzione* on Michelangelo's poetry that he presented to the Florence Academy in 1547. Giorgio Vasari also published it in his *Lives* (1568). The "fair lady" of the second quatrain is probably Vittoria Colonna, Marchesa of Pescara, poetess and friend of the artist, the only one who can understand him. In the first lines Michelangelo expresses his theory of "subtraction" that is the artist physically removes excess material to reveal the existing, shape that was divine-ly created and "hidden" inside the block of marble.

The "thought" or *concetto* in Italian, is a complex and basic term in the Neoplatonic philosophy. It is the image of an artistic subject that is formed in the artist's mind through an almost divine process of inspiration, and he has to try to make it reality to best of his earthy, or hu-man, abilities. In addition the poem reflects the hard effort and frequent bitterness or disappoints of artistic work. They are cryptic lines that have inspired many modern Italian poets such as Montale and Ungaretti.

The best of artists hath no thought to show
What the rough stone in its superfluous shell
Does not include: to break the marble spell
Is all the hand that serves the brain can do.

The ill I shun, the good I seek, even so
In thee, fair lady, proud, ineffable,
Lies hidden: but the art I wield so well
Works against my wish, and lays me low.

Therefore not love, nor thy transcendent face,
Nor cruelty, nor fortune, nor disdain,
Cause my mischance, nor fate, nor destiny;

Since in thy heart thou carries death and grace
Enclosed together, and my worthless brain
Can draw forth only death to feed on me

Non ha l'ottimo artista alcun concetto,
sonnet, 1538/1541–1544;
Florence, Casa Buonarroti, Archivio Buonarroti, inv. XV f. 33a.

MADRIGAL FOR VITTORIA COLONNA

This madrigal was written for Vittoria Colonna to whom Michelangelo frequently dedicated poems from 1536 and 1547. Around 1540 Vittoria, who was also a poet – and friend of Michelangelo – gave him a collection of her spiritual verses, a precious gift since indeed she was adverse to the diffusion of her writings. They exchanged many letters as we learn from Michelangelo himself, but only two of those that he wrote remain. However, many of the poems dedicated to her survive. Often he portrays her as the one capable of transforming the poet's surly character into a work of art. In this madrigal he makes the comparison between the artist who "removes" material to discover a figure inside the hard block of stone, and that is what the woman does by purifying the poet's soul with her words. The insistence on the technique of "removing" that is cutting away the material is typical of Michelangelo's poems: the act becomes a sublimation of the physical. In these lines he expresses the hope that Vittoria Colonna will be able to eliminate her earthly bonds and reveal her inner goodness and purity, almost as a catharsis. Therefore, in the poems for Vittoria Colonna sculpture is a metaphor for the transformation and rebirth achieved by the power of love.

Just as by taking away, lady, one puts
into hard and alpine stone
a figure that's alive
and that grows larger wherever the stone decreases
So too are any good deeds
of the soul that still trembles
concealed by the excess mass of its own flesh
which forms a husk that's coarse and hard.
You alone can still take them out
from within my outer shell
for I have not the will or strength within myself.

Sì come per levar, donna, si pone,
madrigal, 1538–1544;
Florence, Casa Buonarroti, Archivio Buonarroti, inv. XV f. 48b,
from the Baldi Codex.

EPITAPHS FOR CECCHINO BRACCI

In this autograph sheet are four epitaphs Michelangelo wrote in 1544 and sent to Luigi del Riccio. Cecchino Bracci was Del Riccio's beloved nephew who died in Rome that year at the age of fifteen. Michelangelo knew the boy and was fond of him, but it was Del Riccio, Michelangelo's secretary at the time, who asked him to write fifty epitaphs over a few months commemorating the boy. He tempted the artist with offers of fine foods; in a note across the sheet Michelangelo uses the word *ca-castrechi* that means miserly and probably referred to Del Riccio, he signed his name and sketched a crow for the name of the street Macel de' Corvi where he lived in Rome (*Corvo* being the singular for crow in Italian).

It was also Del Riccio who commissioned Michelangelo to design Cecchino's tomb that was erected in the Church of Santa Maria in Aracoeli in Rome during 1545. Sketches conserved in Casa Buonarroti in Florence give us an idea of the design that was modified during construction by Francesco Amatori, known as Urbino. The fourth epitaph expresses the concept of death as a rebirth and the transition from a period of suffering on earth to eternal life in Paradise.

In dying Cecchini has here laid down a corpse
so noble that the sun has never seen its equal.
Rome weeps for him, but heaven smiles with pride
that his soul unburdened of mortal load rejoice.

Here lies Braccio: one could not wish for more
of a tomb for his body, or prayer for his soul.
Since he has a more worthy home dead than alive,
in earth and heaven, death is sweet and kind in him.

Here death stretched out his Arm plucked the unripe
fruit – or rather, the flower, which yields at age fifteen.
Only this rock, which posses him, enjoys him,
while all the rest of the world now weeps for him

I was Cecchin when mortal and now I am divine:
I had little of the world and now enjoy heaven forever.
I rejoice in such a fine change and in death
who gave birth to many others dead, but to me alive.

Epitaphs for Cecchino Bracci,
c. 1544,
Florence, Casa Buonarroti, Archivio Buonarroti, inv. XIII 33.

MADRIGAL ON BLUE PAPER

This witty madrigal is addressed to a woman defined as harsh and beautiful. The lines are enigmatic and the contents difficult to decipher. Michelangelo wants to prove that the woman in question cannot avoid returning his love. With a play of syllogisms he explains his theory in several points. The first clarifies that if beauty is the fruit of a happy soul and vice versa, and this occurs thanks to a harsh and beautiful woman, won't that woman ever want to return his love? He then continues saying that, since at times the woman grumbles saying that his face is ugly because of unhappiness, she is going against her own interests. Indeed, in portraying his beloved, the artist is prompted to paint himself, and if he is unhappy "what can be done?" The conclusion is obvious: it is better to portray one's love happy and without tears washing her face so that she will be beautiful and consequently so will her lover who is reflected in her.

To conclude, Michelangelo continues his games with in a postscript at the bottom of the page, taking the color the paper as his inspiration for the words "Divine things are spoken of in a field of blue" and thus explains his choice of the celeste, blue-gray, color because love is indeed celestial. The madrigal has not been definitively dated, but could have been composed between 1544 and 1546 since it was part of his collection of poems.

If the face grows beautiful from a happy heart
And ugly from a sad one, what will become
of a harsh yet lovely woman
who will not burn for me as I do for her?
For since my bright star made
my eyes quite capable
of distinguishing one beauty from another
that woman is no less cruel
to herself when she often makes
me say, "On account of my heart my face grows dreary,"
For if one portrays himself
in painting a woman, then what
will he make of her if she keeps him unconsoled?
So we'd both do well if I
Could draw her with my heart happy and my face dry
She'd make herself lovely and wouldn't make me ugly.

Se dal cor lieto divien bello il volto,
madrigal, c. 1544–1546;
Florence, Casa Buonarroti, Archivio Buonarroti, inv. XIII 46.

BIBLIOGRAPHY

Given the enormous bibliography on Michelangelo and his works, this bibliography provides some titles for learning more about the artist without any pretense at being exhaustive. The sources listed below, especially the most recent publications, provide additional references.

Two essential **sources** are the biographies written by Giorgio Vasari (1550, 1568) and Ascanio Condivi (1553); we recommend the following editions: G. Vasari, *La vita di Michelangelo*, ed. by P. Barocchi, Milan-Naples 1962; A. Condivi, *Vita di Michelangelo*, the 1550 and 1568 editions, ed. by P. Barocchi, Florence 1998. There are also the following editions of Vasari: G. Vasari, *Le vite de' più eccellenti pittori, scultori et architettori... di nuovo ampliate*, Florence 1568, in *Le opere di Giorgio Vasari*, ed. by G. Milanesi, Florence 1878-1885, 9 vol., I-VII, 1878-1881; G. Vasari, *Le vite de' più eccellenti architetti, pittori et scultori italiani, da Cimabue insino a' tempi nostri*, Florence 1550, ed. by L. Bellosi and A. Rossi, Turin 1986; G. Vasari, *Le vite de' più eccellenti pittori, scultori et architettori nelle redazioni del 1550 e 1568*, Florence 1550 and 1568, ed. by R. Bettarini and P. Barocchi, Florence 1966-1987.

The main and most complete sources for Michelangelo's **letters** and correspondence are: *Il Carteggio di Michelangelo*, ed. by P. Barocchi and R. Ristori, Florence 1965-1983; *Il Carteggio indiretto di Michelangelo*, ed. by P. Barocchi, K. Loach Bramanti, R. Ristori, Florence 1988-1995. An essential source for the **chronology** of Michelangelo's life and works is: K. Weil-Garris Brandt and N. Baldini, *Cronologia ragionata*, in the exhibition catalogue *Giovinezza di Michelangelo*, Florence-Milan 1999, pp. 435-452. R. Hatfield, *The Wealth of Michelangelo*, Rome 2002, is an interesting support on documentary research. **Bibliography** prior to 1927: E. Steinman, R. Wittkover, *Michelangelo-Bibliographie*, I, 1510-1926, Leipzig 1927. One of the fundamental monographs on Michelangelo is: Ch. de Tolnay, *Michelangelo*, Princeton 1943-1960. **General studies** on the artist: Ch. Tolnay, *Michelangiolo*, Florence s.a. [1951]; R. Clements, *Michelangelo. Le idee sull'arte*, Milan 1964, *Michelangelo artista, pensatore, scrittore*, Novara 1965; H. von Einem, *Michelangelo*, Berlin 1973; J. Wilde, *Michelangelo. Six Lectures*, Oxford 1978; R. Salvini, *The Hidden Michelangelo*, Milan-Oxford 1978; L. Heusinger, *Michelangelo*, Antella 1989; B. Nardini, *Michelangelo. Biografia di un genio*, Florence 1999; M. Bussagli, *Michelangelo*, Florence 2000; E.

Crispino, *Michelangelo*, Florence 2001. A. Forcellino, *Michelangelo. Una vita inquieta*, Bari 2005. This is a recent biography. Essays on Michelangelo's **poetic** and interpretations of his work and personality: E. Panofsky, *The Neoplatonic Movement and Michelangelo*, in E. P., Studies in Iconology, New York 1939; D. Summers, *Michelangelo and the Language of Art*, Princeton 1981; R. De Maio, *Michelangelo e la Controriforma*, Florence 1990; G. Spini, *Michelangelo politico e altri studi sul Rinascimento fiorentino*, Milan 1999.

Studies and exhibition catalogues focusing on the artist's **training and early works**: A. Parronchi, *Opere giovanili di Michelangelo*, Florence 1968-2003; *Michelangelo e i maestri del Quattrocento*, ed. by C. Sisi, Florence 1985; *Michelangelo e l'arte classica*, ed. by G. Agosti and V. Farinella, Florence 1987; G. C. Argan, B. Contardi, *Michelangelo*, in "Art e dossier" n. 9, Florence 1991; *Il disegno fiorentino del tempo di Lorenzo il Magnifico*, exhibition catalogue ed. by A. M. Petrioli Tofani, Cinisello Balsamo (Milan) 1992; *Il giardino di San Marco. Maestri e compagni del giovane Michelangelo*, ed. by P. Barocchi, Cinisello Balsamo (Milan) 1992; M. Hirst-J. Dunkerton, *Making and Meaning. The Young Michelangelo*, London 1994; C. Acidini Luchinat, E. Capretti, K. Weil-Garris Brandt, *Michelangelo. Gli anni giovanili*, in "Art e dossier" n. 150, Florence 1999; *Giovinezza di Michelangelo*, exhibition catalogue (Florence), ed. by K. Weil-Garris Brandt, C. Acidini Luchinat, J. D.

Draper, N. Penny, Florence-Milan 1999; *D'après l'antique*, exhibition catalogue ed. by J.-P. Cuzin, J.-R. Gaborit et al., Paris 2000.

The following titles deal with Michelangelo's arts.

Sculpture: P. Barocchi, *Finito e non-finito nella critica vasariana*, in "Arte Antica e Moderna", 1958, n. 3, pp. 221-235; J. Schulz, *Michelangelo's Unfinished Work*, in "The Art Bulletin", LVII, 1975, pp. 366-373; *L'opera completa di Michelangelo scultore*, ed. by U. Baldini, Milan 1973; C. Echinger-Maurach, *Studien zu Michelangelos Juliusgrabmal*, Olms 1991; J. Beck, A. Paolucci, B. Santi, *Un occhio su Michelangelo: le tombe dei Medici nelle sagrestia nuova di S. Lorenzo a Firenze dopo il restauro*, Bergamo 1993; G. Cosmo, *Michelangelo. La scultura*, in "Art e dossier" n. 125, Florence 1997; A. Paolucci, *Michelangelo: le Pietà*, Milan 1997; *Il Crocifisso di Santo Spirito - The Crucifix of Santo Spirito*, ed. by Comune di Firenze, Assessorato alla Cultura, Florence 2000; *L'"Adolescente" dell'Ermitage e la Sagrestia Nuova di Michelangelo*, exhibition catalogue (Florence) ed. by S. Androsov and U. Baldini, Siena 2000; S. Danesi Squarzina, *The Bassano "Christ the Redeemer" in the Giustiniani Collection*, in "The Burlington Magazine", CXLII, 2000, pp. 746-751; A. Forcellino, *Michelangelo Buonarroti, storia di una passione eretica*, Turin 2002; J. Wasserman, *Michelangelo's Florence Pietà*, Princeton - Oxford 2003; *Exploring David. Diagnostic Tests and State of Conservation*, ed. by S. Bracci, F. Falletti, M. Matteini, R. Scopigno,

Florence 2004; M. T. Fiorio, *La Pietà Rondanini*, Milan 2004; A. Paolucci, G. M. Radke, F. Falletti, *Michelangelo: il David*, in "Art e dossier" n. 202, Florence 2004; *Proposta per Michelangelo giovane. Un Crocifisso in legno di tiglio*, exhibition catalogue (Florence) ed. by G. Gentilini, Turin 2004; *Il David di Michelangelo: storia e restauro*, Florence 2004; G. Donati, *Michelangelo*, Rome 2005; C. Acidini Luchinat, *Michelangelo scultore*, Milan 2005.

Architecture: *Michelangelo architetto*, ed. by P. Portoghesi and B. Zevi, Turin 1964; J. Ackerman, *L'architettura di Michelangelo*, Turin 1968; *Disegni di fortificazioni da Leonardo a Michelangelo*, exhibition catalogue ed. by P.C. Marani, Florence 1984; H. A. Millon and C. H. Smyth , *Michelangelo architetto: la facciata di San Lorenzo e la cupola di San Pietro*; exhibition catalogue (Florence), Milan 1988; G. C. Argan, B. Contardi, *Michelangelo architetto*, Milan 1990; San Lorenzo: 393 - 1993. *L'architettura. Le vicende della fabbrica*, exhibition catalogue ed. by G. Morolli and P. Ruschi, Florence 1993; *La difficile eredità. Architettura a Firenze dalla Repubblica all'assedio*, exhibition catalogue ed. by M. Dezzi Bardeschi, Florence 1994.

Painting: *L'opera completa di Michelangelo pittore*, ed. by E. Camesasca, Milan 1966; R. Longhi, *Breve ma veridica storia della pittura italiana*, Florence 1980; *La Cappella sistina. I primi restauri: la scoperta del colore*, Novara 1986; *Michelangelo e la Sistina. La tecnica, il restauro, il mito*, exhibition catalogue, Rome 1990; *La Cappella Sistina. La volta restaurata: il trionfo del colore*, Novara 1992; *Michelangelo, la Cappella Sistina: documentazione e interpretazioni*, Vatican City 1994-1999; A. Natali, *La piscina Betsaide. Movimenti nell'arte fiorentina del Cinquecento*, Florence-Siena 1995; L. Partridge, *Michelangelo: la volta della Cappella Sistina*, Turin 1996; M. Calvesi, *La Cappella Sistina e la sua decorazione da Perugino a Michelangelo*, Rome, 1997; P. L. De Vecchi, *La Cappella Sistina. Il Giudizio Universale*, Milan 1997; *La Cappella Sistina: il Giudizio restaurato*, Novara 1998; S. Zuffi, *Michelangelo. La Cappella Sistina*, Milan 1999; *La Sistina e Michelangelo. Storia e fortuna di un capolavoro*, exhibition catalogue ed. by A. De Strobel and G. Gentili, Milan 2003; C. Gamba, *Michelangelo*, Milan 2004; C. Acidini Luchinat, *Michelangelo pittore*, Milan (in press).

Drawings: J. Wilde, *Italian Drawings in the Department of Prints and Drawings in the British Museum. Michelangelo and his Studio*, London 1953; P. Barocchi, *Michelangelo e la sua scuola. I disegni di Casa Buonarroti e degli Uffizi*, exhibition catalogue, Florence 1962; P. Barocchi, *Michelangelo e la sua scuola. I disegni dell'archivio Buonarroti*, Florence 1964; F. Hartt, *The Drawings of Michelangelo*, London 1971; *Il tondo Doni di Michelangelo e il suo restauro*, Florence 1985, in "Gli Uffizi. Studi e ricerche"; C. de Tolnay, *Corpus dei disegni di Michelangelo*, Novara 1975-1980; *I disegni murali di Michelangiolo e della sua scuola nella Sagrestia Nuova di San Lorenzo*, ed. by Paolo Dal Poggetto, Florence 1979;

Disegni di fortificazioni da Leonardo a Michelangelo, exhibition catalogue ed. by P. C. Marani, Florence 1984; M. Hirst, *Michelangelo and His Drawings*, New Haven - London 1988; *Miche-langelo Drawings* (Proceedings of the Symposium, Center for Advanced Study in the Visual Arts, Washington, 7-8 October 1988), ed. by C. H. Smyth, Washington 1992, in "Studies in the History of Art", XXXIII, 1992; J. Joannides, *Michel-Ange: élèves et copistes*, with V. Goarin and C. Scheck, Paris 2003.

Poetry: Michelangelo Buonarroti, *Rime*, ed. by Enzo Noé Girardi, Bari 1960; E. N. Girardi, *La critica letter-aria su Michelangelo*, in Conference Proceedings "Convegno di studi mi-chelangioleschi nel IV Centenario del-la morte del Maestro"; E. N. Girardi, *Studi su Michelangelo scrittore*, Flor-ence 1974; V. Binni, *Michelangelo scrittore*, Turin 1975; M. Buonarroti, *Rime*, ed. by M. Residori, Milan 1998.

Catalogues from recent exhibitions: *The Genius of the Sculptor in Miche-langelo's Work*, exhibition catalogue, Montreal 1992; *L'ombra del genio. Michelangelo e l'arte classica a Firenze 1537-1631*, exhibition catalogue ed. by M. Chiarini, A. P. Darr, C. Gian-nini (Florence-Chicago-Detroit); Mi-lan 2002; *Michelangelo e Dante*, exhi-bition catalogue ed. by C. Gizzi, Milan 1995; *Michelangelo: grafia e biografia di un genio*, exhibition catalogue (Milan) ed. by L. Bardeschi Ciulich; *Michelangelo: grafia e bi-ografia. Disegni e autografi del maestro*, exhibition catalogue (Rome- Biel-Bienne) ed. by L. Bardeschi Ciulich

and P. Ragionieri, Florence 2002; *Mi-chelangelo nell'Ottocento. Il centenario del 1875*, exhibition catalogue (Flor-ence) ed. by C. Sisi, Milan 1994; *Michelangelo nell'Ottocento: Rodin e Michelangelo*, exhibition catalogue (Florence-Philadelphia), Milan 1996; *L'officina della maniera. Varietà e fie-rezza nell'arte fiorentina del Cinque-cento fra le due repubbliche 1494-1530*, exhibition catalogue (Florence) ed. by A. Cecchi and A. Natali, Venice 1996; *Vita di Michelangelo*, exhibition cata-logue (Florence) ed. by L. Bardeschi Ciulich and P. Ragionieri, Florence 2001; *Venere e Amore. Michelangelo e la nuova bellezza ideale - Venus and Love. Michelangelo and the new ideal of beau-ty*, exhibition catalogue ed. by F. Fal-letti and J.K. Nelson, Florence 2002; *Michelangelo tra Firenze e Roma*, exhi-bition catalogue (Rome-Siracusa) ed. by P. Ragionieri, Florence 2003; *Daniele da Volterra, amico di Miche-langelo*, exhibition catalogue ed. by V. Romani, Florence 2003; *Vittoria Colonna e Michelangelo*, exhibition catalogue ed. by P. Ragionieri, Flor-ence 2005.

On Michelangelo's **funeral:** *The Divine Michelangelo: The Florentine Academy's Homage on his Death in 1564*, ed. by R. and M. Wittkover, London 1964.